# REFIT ANNUAL
# 2002

# Refit Annual 2002

is published by

EDISEA LIMITED

a subsidiary of

Boat International Publications Limited

5-7 Kingston Hill, Kingston upon Thames

Surrey KT2 7PW, England

Tel: +44 (0)20 8547 2662

Fax: +44 (0)20 8547 1201

| | |
|---|---|
| Publisher | Christian Chalmin |
| Editor | David Pelly |
| Consulting Editor | Amanda McCracken |
| Managing Editor | Lucinda Roch |
| Design | Francesca Bechara |
| Production Manager | Francis Ransom |
| Production Assistant | Samantha Collins |
| Sales Director | Malcolm MacLean |
| Advertisement Manager | Charles Finney |
| Advertisement Sales | Douglas Hunter |
| | Geoff Jones, Amy Merrigan |
| Advertisement Designer | Tom Cole |
| Advertisement Coordinator | Heidi Parrott |

ISBN 1 898524 114

British Library Cataloguing-in-Publication Data
A catalogue record for this book is available from
the British Library

Printed by Markono Print Media Pte Ltd, Singapore.
Origination by Graphic Facilities, London

# Dry your tears.

## Our Team will comfort you ...with Repair, Refit or Conversion.

If you want a reliable yard handling your yacht with outstanding care, and if you are looking for the finest facilities in conjunction with awarm and traditional hospitality, then you´ve found us. Lürssen: your home away from home.

Bremen has been renowned for centuries as a hospitable and open-minded town, which provides you with many possibilities for first class dining, leisure and entertainment near the Lürssen Shipyard.

...it´s time for **LÜRSSEN**

# Contents

## Refit Annual 2002

# Foreword

Growing up in Newark, New Jersey, is not the easiest place to develop a love of classic racing yachts. Fortunately, Tyco International, the company that I now serve as chairman, is based in Bermuda and headquartered in New Hampshire – locations where it is easier to satisfy my passion.

I first became interested in yachts many years ago, as a young boy at the Jersey Shore. Over the years, my interest developed into a passion as I learnt more about the history of this sport, and I became increasingly focused on racing classic yachts.

Having raced these vessels for several years now, it is clear to me that there are basically two types of sailors. First, there are those who seek the pleasure of speed for speed's sake. Frankly, they are welcome to their modern yachts, using every trick that technology offers to create more aerodynamic lines, greater acceleration and pace.

I am unashamedly an enthusiastic member of the second group. We are people who combine our love of speed and racing with an appreciation for style and for the effort that skilled craftspeople put into reconditioning classic yachts, giving them a new lease of life.

To me, refitted classic yachts are the only way to enjoy racing at its finest. With what other sailing vessel can a team of trained racers be surrounded by a proud tradition and heritage, even as they push themselves to the limit physically and mentally? How else can you simultaneously enjoy the speed of a perfectly designed yacht, while marvelling at its beauty?

Two years ago, I became the owner of *Endeavour*. To me, she is the epitome of everything that a J-Class is: elegant, charismatic and luxurious, but also a vessel that possesses great strength and speed. Participating in races at the helm of *Endeavour* is a very special and unique experience.

To me, *Endeavour*'s restoration is a perfect illustration of why refitting classic yachts has become so popular. In bringing a classic back to life, dedicated specialists have recreated a magnificent yacht, updating it while remaining true to the original designer and the first owner.

I am particularly excited that, as this edition of *Refit Annual* shows, the movement to restore these great sailing ships has grown by leaps and bounds. Indeed, with the completion of the *Shamrock V* restoration, one of the feature articles in this year's annual, there will be three active J-Class yachts – a great accomplishment, as there were only 10 ever built.

With each refitted classic, more and more lucky sailors have the opportunity to share in our enjoyment and appreciate these classics for what they truly are – works of art that can really move!

**L. Dennis Kozlowski**

# Introduction

The 150th anniversary of the original race for the America's Cup has been the catalyst for a new surge of activity in yacht restoration during the past year. For anyone with more than a passing interest in classic yachts, the great gathering at Cowes in August 2001 was an occasion not to be missed and one at which every classic yacht had to be in tip-top condition. It provided the impetus for the total restoration of the J-Class cutter *Shamrock V*, which we report in this edition of *Refit Annual*, in addition to a huge amount of work on other yachts.

During the three years that *Refit Annual* has been published, the yacht refit industry has matured considerably with an increasing degree of specialization becoming apparent. At one extreme we find large shipyards such as Devonport Yachts, which are able to undertake major engineering tasks on vessels of any size, and at the other small companies such as JFA, which can spend two years completing a single high-quality refit.

Perhaps even more significant in the long term has been the emergence of companies such as Amico in Italy or Derecktor of Florida, which carry out a large number of refits and repairs every year on time and on budget. It is tempting to class such refits as 'routine' but actually no refit is routine as each and every job throws up its own list of problems to be overcome, many of which cannot be foreseen. This is why good management is paramount in refit work. When a vessel is opened up and a variety of complications become apparent, it is fatally easy for the work programme to run out of control, with tradesmen of every kind falling over each other and regulation of costs being lost.

There is one task that is common to virtually every refit job – painting, and it is difficult for the layman to understand just what a major undertaking it is to repaint a large yacht. In this edition of *Refit Annual* we are privileged to have two of the best-known names in the industry, Pinmar and US Paints, join forces to give a fascinating insight into their work. Once again it turns out to be a mixture of skill and management, each one being useless without the other.

One enterprise that was launched with all flags flying at the same time as this publication and has unfortunately not survived is the Refit Show in Palma. It turned out to have been in the wrong place at the wrong time as it clashed with other events in the increasingly busy calendar. It may be that the refit industry will find another way of setting out its stall in the future but for the time being *Refit Annual* is the best showcase available and a role we are very proud to fill.

*David Pelly*

**DAVID PELLY**
**Editor**

# SUPERYACHT REFIT IN GENOA
## www.amico.it

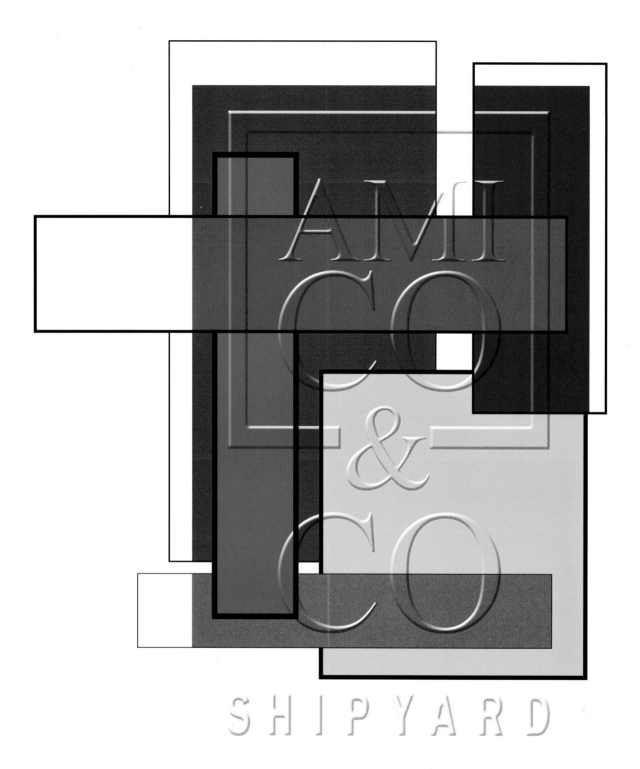

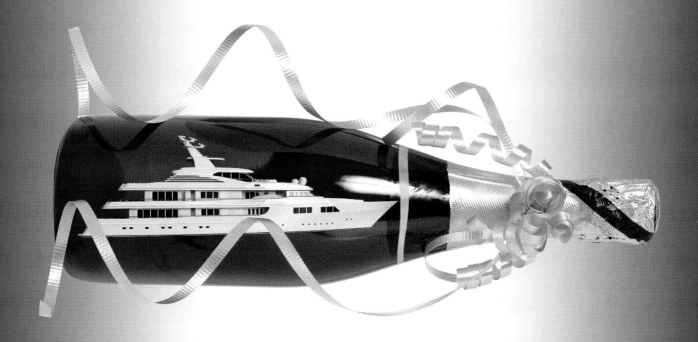

**WORLD CLASS YACHTS
WORLD CLASS REFITS.**

LEANDER

VIRGINIAN

SOUTHERN CROSS III

TALITHA G

Devonport has all the resources, experience and expertise needed for major yacht refits. With a new way of working and a new attitude to excellence, you can rely on us for even the most complex projects. For world class work, talk to a yard with yachtspertise.

eVolution

ReVolution

**DEVONPORT**

DEVONPORT YACHTS  PLYMOUTH PL1 4SG  UK  T: +44 (0)1752 323213  F: +44 (0)1752 323247  E: YACHTS@DEVONPORT.CO.UK

# Opulent, yet Intimate

Imagine if you can, a true mega-yacht packaged
in an eighty-foot hull. Imagine if you can, complete privacy
in a yacht of this size, where crew can go about their business
without ever being noticed. This is the very lap of luxury,
in a setting as comfortable as your living room.
Welcome your family and your friends aboard
your private estate at sea, and savor these moments
knowing genius is truly hereditary.

**Azimut S.p.A.**, Via M.L. King 9-11, 10051 Avigliana (Turin - Italy)
Tel.: (+39) 011 93.161, Fax: (+39) 011 936.72.70, www.azimutyachts.net

Powered by **mtu**

**KOHLER**
GENERATORS
POWER
ON DEMAND

80

AZIMUT

Live the
Italian Renaissance

**KVH, the leader in mobile satellite antenna technology, presents TracVision & Tracphone, bringing you 300+ channels of premiere digital satellite TV and crystal-clear phone/fax/data service wherever you go!!**

Satellite Antenna Systems

TracVision®/Tracphone®

# KVH®

*Keeping Track of Your World*

**KVH Industries, Inc.**
50 Enterprise Center • Middletown, RI 02842 • U.S.A.
Phone: +1 401 847 3327 • Fax: +1 401 849 0045
E-mail: info@kvh.com

**Visit us at www.kvh.com**

**KVH Europe A/S**
Ved Klaedebo 12 • 2970 Hoersholm • Denmark
Phone: +45 45 160 180 • Fax: +45 45 867 077
E-mail: info@kvh.dk

775 Taylor Lane,   Dania,   FL 33004
Tel: 954 920-5756   Fax: 954 925-1146
Email: millert@derecktor-florida.com
w w w . d e r e c k t o r - f l o r i d a . c o m

# DERECKTOR OF FLORIDA
## Since 1967

At Derecktor of Florida, Inc. our mission is quite simple –
advanced design, and high quality which exceed customer's
expectations.

**Specializing in refit and repair of all types of vessels.**

Derecktor of Florida's 17 acre facility is the best
equipped shipyard in the state of Florida, capable
of handling motor and sailing yachts up to 600 tons
and currently servicing yachts up to 315 feet.
With our future expansion, we will be able to lift
and service vessels up to 3000 tons.

# Peter Allan & Flip Thomsen provide a commonsense approach to a major
# Repainting project

**PINMAR S.A.**
YACHT PAINTING SYSTEMS

**PAINT SCHEDULE**

**M.Y. SUPERYACHT**

| MONTHS / WORKS TO BE CARRIED OUT | Jan 2001 | Feb 2001 | Mar 2001 | Apr 2001 | May 2001 |
|---|---|---|---|---|---|
| Shipyard remove caulking lines | ■ | | | | |
| Scaffolding and protective tent erection | ■ | | | | |
| Removal of fittings | ■ | | | | |
| Protective masking | ■ | | | | |
| Degreasing of paint surfaces | | ■ | | | |
| Cut out blister repairs | | ■ | | | |
| General sanding | | ■ | | | |
| Application of High Build Primer | | ■ | | | |
| General sanding of High Build Primer | | | ■ | | |
| Application of 545 primer | | | ■ | | |
| General sanding for topcoats | | | ■ | | |
| Wash down entire vessel | | | ■ | | |
| Remasking of entire vessel | | | ■ | | |
| Final topcoating of hardware | | | ■ | | |
| Final topcoating on board | | | | ■ | |
| Remounting of fittings on hardware | | | | ■ | |
| Remounting of fittings on board | | | | | ■ |
| Remove protective tent and scaffolding | | | | | ■ |
| Apply non skid | | | | | ■ |
| Final touch ups and general cleaning | | | | | ■ |
| Shipyard re-apply caulking | | | | | ■ |
| Vessel to depart Palma | | | | | ■ |

This article is not designed to teach anyone how to paint a yacht, but rather to suggest a general approach for supervisory staff and project managers and to give owners and captains an insight into what is involved. No attempt has been made to write a technical manual, which would demand its own dedicated book. First, there are some basic criteria to be established if the end result is to meet or even exceed expectations:-

1. Determine the exact scope of work involved

2. Determine the project time required and whether the yacht can be made available for that amount of time

3. Determine which, if any, non-painting works are planned during the same period

4. Determine the on-site conditions necessary

The scope of work involved should be established before seeking quotations to ensure that each yard or contractor is quoting apples against apples. All too often companies bidding for the work establish their offer on their own appraisal of what is required, leaving the client with the task of

deciphering the differences. It saves everyone's time and money if all quotations are based upon a predetermined specification and scope of work.

When someone buys a yacht with the intention of carrying out a major refit, they will normally be advised by brokers, designers and other professionals. However, establishing the stability of the existing coating system and setting a full technical specification is a speciality in itself. At Pinmar, we work closely with Joop Ellenbroek of CCS Yacht Coating Services in Holland, who will test existing coatings, specify the treatment required and oversee the painting project on behalf of the owner. Often the choice of which brand of paint is to be used is taken by the yacht owner or captain and, when an independent consultant is not involved, it is usually left to the painting contractor to recommend a specification.

Film thicknesses and application procedures vary between makers and when a paint manufacturer is selected, one should contact their technical department for advice and application requirements. If the specification calls for the use of a paint other than that already applied to the yacht, a series of tests is required to establish whether or not the old coating system will accept the change to a different product:-

1. Cross hatch adhesion test
2. Solvent resistance test
3. Coating compatibility test

Any competent painting contractor should be able to do these tests.

The project time required does not always match the period for which the yacht can be made available and all too frequently painting companies will commit to a blatantly impossible schedule. Throwing 40 painters at a project that would normally require a team of 12 or 15 is not going to solve the problem. Also, the chemical products used in today's coating systems have drying and curing periods that must be respected if they are to give the performance required. Their successful use requires a degree of professional skill that not every 'painter' possesses. Cutting short the process or using a large amount of labour of doubtful skill is a certain recipe for a disappointing result.

When referring to the word application it encompasses the entire process including preparation, filling, sanding and so forth. Using unskilled labour for any of this process will cause problems. Projects which run past their deadlines are of course unacceptable, but so are poor results caused by trying to do too much in too little time. The demand for truly skilled applicators far outweighs the supply, so beware of any company suddenly producing a much larger than usual labour force.

One of the most common causes of delays and poor results is attempting to carry out non-painting works such as carpentry, deck laying, caulking and lifting capping rails during the time period allowed for painting. Ideally the painters should have the exterior of the yacht to themselves, but we don't live in a perfect world and we must therefore adapt to the reality of the situation. Coordination with other trades is therefore paramount or the outcome of the entire project will be prejudiced.

**Below left:** a 55m (180ft) yacht, complete with scaffolding and plastic cover

**Above:** the topsides of the yachts, covered in brown paper

**Below:** when sanding edges, always apply some tape to protect the adjacent surfaces

**Bottom:** on major projects it is often necessary to skim fair complete areas over the old paint system

Some activities must not be permitted when painting, as anyone who has seen the contamination caused by oily teak dust and caulking compounds will bear witness. However provided there is flexibility and understanding on both sides, apparently conflicting activities can be carried out during the same project period.

The working environment is obviously crucial to the outcome, but it is rare indeed to execute a refit/repaint in ideal conditions. Even top yards constructing new yachts can rarely offer the perfect environment, so we must create the best on-site conditions possible. If the yacht is outside and will remain in the water throughout the project, we assume that it is moored in a relatively warm climate and not in northern Europe. The environment can be controlled by erecting on board scaffolding which is then shrink-wrapped in plastic, complete with filters for fresh air input and extraction. Also, the hull topsides can be prepared and painted from special rafts designed for the job, although this is only applicable for the larger yachts as smaller craft do not have the clearance between the water level and the top of the boot top. Care must be taken to avoid any salt water splashing up and paint application can only really be carried out when there is no wind – so make sure you pick your day. If in a shed within a yard, the only thing that differs is the scaffolding being mounted from the shop floor. The cover is still needed to avoid contamination and heating may also be required to control the humidity level under the cover. So assuming the above four points have been successfully organized, let's look at the task at hand.

The first objective is to set a production schedule for each part of the process in each area of the boat, taking into account the other craftsmen that need to work aboard. At Pinmar we start with an overall bar chart and, once satisfied that it is a practical

schedule, we then prepare a bar chart for each area. These charts are displayed so as to be available to everyone working on the project.

The first task is a thorough inspection for any existing damage to the vessel. We normally walk around with the mate or the bosun looking for items such as scratched windows and fittings, damage or staining to teak rails, decks, varnish works and so forth. Once noted and signed off, often with supporting photographs, we are then assured that no dispute will arise at the end of the job.

Assuming the boat is washed and dry, several things happen at once during the first few days of the project. Painters will start taping and covering to protect items such as glass, decks and handrails. Riggers, or sometimes the crew, will dismantle fittings and carpenters will, if required, remove the caulking compound where the teak decks and handrails butt up to painted surfaces. This is to allow the painters access to the source of any corrosion present and to ensure an unbroken paint film to below deck level. It will also guarantee a perfect seal when the caulking seam is reinstated following completion of painting. When a given area is considered ready for the basic preparation to start, which involves all fittings being removed and all residue of the deck caulking cleaned up, the first job is to solvent wipe the painted surfaces to remove any remaining residue or other contaminants. Next we open up any blisters, cracks and defects in the existing coating. For the purposes of this article we will assume that grit-blasting is not required and spot repairs will suffice.

The root of most blistering or cracking can be exposed by the careful use of small air grinders – 'careful' because over-enthusiastic grinding may well obscure the cause. On new builds and refits carried out in the last 10 years, the cause may not always be corrosion. Due to the ever-increasing

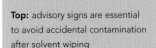

**Top:** advisory signs are essential to avoid accidental contamination after solvent wiping

**Above:** old fairing bevelled back to ensure good adhesion of the new fairing compound

**Right:** solvent wiping Awlgrip High Build prior to applying the final primer coat

pressure on time, too many of the products used in the fairing and painting process are being incorrectly applied and the curing times are not respected. This is resulting in surface defects which have countless possible causes, the more common ones being:-

1. Undercured fairing compound, which can be the entire substrate or previous repair spots

2. Poorly mixed fairing compound resulting in individual spots of pure base component or hardener

3. Poorly applied fairing compound resulting in air pockets within the individual layers

4. Primers that are applied unevenly or too thickly, causing solvent entrapment

5. Incorrect film thickness of primers and topcoats

Assuming we are dealing with normal corrosion causing blistering and we have ground out the blistered or cracked area, we then need to establish whether any substrate repair is required due to a crack or severe pitting in the corroded area. This is subsequently corrected by welding, or lay-up repair in the case of a laminated structure, and we can then proceed with the painting process. It is very important that the surrounding edge to the repair spot is bevelled back from the area to be faired. A minimum of 6 to 1 gradient, preferably more, is required to ensure a good bond between the existing fairing compound and the fairing compound to be applied.

However first we want to prime the exposed area of metal, and we shall presume that we are using the Awlgrip Coating System and that our yacht was originally faired and painted using the same system. Dealing with a mixed system from various manufacturers would call for a book of its own. It is important to use the same fairing compound used originally because different brands have varying degrees of hardness and a softer or harder filler may cause 'mapping out', where a fine line highlights the repair and prints through the topcoat. Prior to initial priming of the repair spots, the metal substrate must be clean and abraded.

We do not use acid-based metal preparation products on repair patches as they can infiltrate under the existing coatings and also be absorbed by the open filler around the repair spot. A thorough clean using Awlgrip T0006 or T0002 and clean cotton rags is sufficient. As the open filler will absorb the cleaning solvent, allow two to three hours for its evaporation prior to priming.

The first primer is not only to protect the metal and avoid corrosion, it also acts as a glue to stick the fairing compound to the surface, so it is crucial to the stability of the entire coating system. The application of primer in repair spots is best carried out using a small spray gun to control the film thickness. The manufacturer's recommended dry film thickness (DFT) should remain in place after sanding

**Top left and right:** skim fairing the topsides in the water. The clearance required from the waterline to the top of the boot top is very evident

**Above left:** this type of complete cover is often used inside large hangars to avoid local contamination

**Below:** apply the fairing compound in multiple fine coats in order to avoid air entrapment

**Right:** the wash down prior to retaping for the topcoat application on *Limitless* in the Pinmar shed at Barcelona

**Below:** apply the first sealer coat over the fairing compound by roller

**Bottom:** the applicator uses a wet film thickness gauge while spray applying Awlgrip High Build coats

or the product cannot be expected to do its job.

We prime using Awlgrip Hullguard ER to a DFT of 75 microns (mcs). This product does not require sanding if faired over within eight weeks, but we always run a Scotchbrite scouring pad over it to be sure. The filling and fairing process for spot repairs is no different to fairing a larger area in as much as correct mixing, avoidance of air entrapment and so forth are equally important. Apply the Awlgrip LW filler in relatively thin multiple coats, working it to expel air bubbles, and leave it slightly proud of the surrounding surface. Allow it to cure for a minimum of 72 hours at 20 degrees centigrade prior to sanding and sealing with primer, or longer in cooler temperatures. If you cut short this

initial curing time you will have problems later.

When sanding the new filler in the repair spots, use a sanding board such as that produced by 3M. It is faster to use a DA (double action) sanding machine, but not all 'painters' are proficient at using it when sanding filled patches.

The Awlgrip LW Fairing Compound is of a relatively closed texture, so we do not require a finishing filler. However, after sanding we apply a final fine coat, under pressure, in order to fill any surface pores which may have been left. This is called a 'resin coat' and should not, if applied correctly, require much if any sanding.

To seal the newly applied fairing compound you have a selection of epoxy primers. A popular choice in Europe is the Awlgrip Ultra Build D8008 Epoxy Primer, but we prefer Awlgrip High Build D9002 Yellow Epoxy Primer because it contains chromate which is highly anticorrosive and, if the repair filler has been sanded through, this product will protect the high points of metal. Chromate is on its way out, but until it is banned, it is hard to ignore its effectiveness. Apply the first coat by roller to fill any pinholes in the fairing compound.

Now we are ready to sand all general surfaces in preparation for intermediate primer, so using 220 grit sandpaper, we sand the old paint to a totally matt finish and thoroughly clean up all sanding residue. We then apply a full coat, minimum two passes, wet on wet, of Awlgrip 545 Epoxy Primer D8001 to a DFT of 75 to 85mcs, allowing sufficient time between passes for solvent evaporation. This should leave at least 50 to 55mcs after sanding. To sand the primer we do one pass with 220 grit paper to remove any minor 'orange peel' effect, followed by 320 grit to eliminate scratches that would print through. Remember to solvent wipe the primer prior to sanding, using the two cloth method to remove any dirty hand-marks that may have appeared while waiting for the primer to harden.

It is now time for a really major clean up, including the removal of all masking tape and plastic used as protection, followed by a full wash down. We have all seen painters try to reduce this work by putting new protection over the old, and with predictable dusty results. If this project is using a shrink wrap plastic covering then this must be pressure washed along with the scaffolding. In some cases we remove and replace the shrink wrap with new plastic. Expensive yes, but cheaper than having to repaint the yacht because of dust.

When all new masking and plastic has been put on, it is time for the first solvent wipe to remove any contaminants that may have arrived on the surface during re-taping and re-covering. Once the first paint shoot is decided, the rest of the primed areas of the yacht must be covered and protected from overspray. When the last solvent wipe of the areas to be painted in this first shoot is carried out, the final check for any minor surface defects can be done. The secret to any good paint job is to check, check, then check again.

For the application of topcoats the watchword is cleanliness, so no other tradesmen, no crew members and not one single person who is not absolutely essential to the shoot should be on board. Try to plan the application so that the applicators are in the area of fresh paint for the absolute minimum of time. This includes preventing them from having a long walk past fresh paint while carrying all their equipment to get off the yacht once they have finished painting.

The actual mixing of the paint, be it primers or topcoats, needs to be tightly controlled. The basic blend of components is stipulated by the coatings manufacturer, but local conditions vary enormously

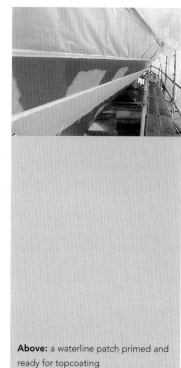

**Above:** a waterline patch primed and ready for topcoating

**Below:** the upper part of the topsides is now completed and will be covered while spraying the lower section

**Above:** yachts under cover for painting by Pinmar in Barcelona

**Below and bottom:** protecting finished areas from overspray. Scaffold poles close to the painted surface should always be covered to avoid dusty surprises when spraying

and must be taken into account with every paint mix. One fundamental rule is to check the batch numbers of all topcoat containers and if you do not have enough of the same batch to paint the entire yacht as well as 20 per cent in reserve, then mix all the colour bases together and re-can them, so that one area of paint does not have a different tone of colour to another. Colour can and does vary slightly from batch to batch, so do not take any chances.

Now we are ready to start applying the topcoats, so the applicators are all in brand new paper or plastic overalls, with new head and shoe covers, all air and fluid hoses/lines are in place aboard and, if they have been used before, they are wrapped in clean plastic, and the spraymen's assistants are slowly wiping down with 'tack rags'. The objective is to apply Awlgrip Gloss Topcoat to a DFT of 50 to 75mcs and to achieve this will require a minimum of three coats applied wet on wet.

Everybody has their own technique when applying topcoat and it is not uncommon to see six or eight skilled painters all using slightly different methods. The important thing is that the application is successful. To achieve the film build required, each of the coats will need time to dry sufficiently so that it can support the following coat. The duration required depends upon local conditions, especially temperature, but we prefer a minimum of one hour between coats and longer on a cool day.

Throughout the application process, the assistants will be using wet film thickness gauges to control the film build. These plastic gauges do get attacked by solvents and should be replaced frequently. Also

we locate control panels in the masking adjacent to the painted surfaces to enable us to check actual DFT following application, without resorting to destructive testing of the finished area.

Each area of the yacht will be topcoated in the same way, covering the fresh paint when dry enough to do so, but at the same time being careful not to cover in a way that allows plastic sheeting direct contact with fresh paint. We use brown paper first, then plastic, with just enough slack to allow air circulation between the paint and brown paper.

Repainting yachts requires a certain discipline and the supervision of all aspects of the project is crucial if the desired result is to be attained. Only a fool would call it easy to achieve, but by taking a commonsense approach and sticking to the basic criteria, many frequently seen disappointments can be avoided.

Peter Allan is President of Pinmar SA

Contramuelle Mollet 6, 07012

Palma de Mallorca, Spain

Tel:+34 971 713 744

Fax:+34 971 718 143

Flip Thomsen is Managing Director

of US Paint Europe

Bouwelven 1, Industrieszone – Kleingent, B-2280

Grobbendonk, Belgium

Tel:+32 14 230001

Fax:+32 14 230880

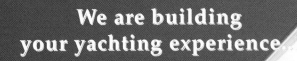

# Think you've
# seen
#### it all...

# Well
# Think Again!

Image is a representation.

 **INFRARED**™

# See what you've been Missing!

# The first 15m class racing for 85 years

Photo: Franco Pace

*Tuiga* **and** *The Lady Anne* **restored by Fairlie Restorations**

Other yachts to benefit from this treatment include:
*Kentra, Fulmar, Belle Aventure, Carron II* **and** *Siris*

Fairlie Restorations Ltd. are the custodians
of the William Fife Archive

**FAIRLIE RESTORATIONS LTD**
UNIT 4, PORT HAMBLE, SATCHELL LANE, HAMBLE, HAMPSHIRE SO31 4NN
TEL: +44(0) 23 8045 6336  FAX: +44(0) 23 8045 6166  EMAIL:Info@fairlierestorations.com

# AWLGRIP.®

## Helping ⬚LADIES⬚

## look their best.

For years, refit yards have turned to AWLGRIP® coating systems to protect the world's finest yachts. And with good reason. AWLGRIP® is the unchallenged leader in urethane topcoats. With its superior resistance to sun, saltwater, chemicals and abrasion, AWLGRIP® is ideal for coating everything from topsides, cabin tops, decks and masts to engines. It's just one of a complete line of products by U.S. Paint that, when used as a complete system, provide chemically cured finishes resistant to abrasion, chalking, corrosion and chemical attack. For more information, U.S. Tel: 314.621.0525, Intl. Tel: 32.14.230001 or visit **www.uspaint.com**

**AWLGRIP®**

**U.S. PAINT**
CORPORATION

WE COVER THE WORLD'S FINEST YACHTS

# THE
# YACHTS

# Istranka

**Above:** built originally in 1952 for the President of Yugoslavia, Josef Broz Tito, *Istranka* now combines classic looks with modern comforts, making her the ideal ocean cruising yacht

**Right:** the continuation of *Istranka*'s refit was coordinated by shipping agents and brokers, EEC Shipping

The 45.6m (149ft 8in) motor yacht *Istranka* has suffered what is euphemistically known as a 'colourful history.' The pinnacle of her career was in the 1960s when she was the state yacht of Yugoslavia and world leaders walked her decks. The deepest trough came in the early 1980s when she was sold at public auction in Monte Carlo because the harbour authorities wanted to get rid of her. Today she is a virtually brand new classic yacht which has been totally rebuilt and re-equipped from stem to stern.

Between the two lies a long story which we only have space to touch on briefly. Although it is not certain whether she was built as a yacht or converted to one, it is clear that *Istranka*'s hull was one of a class of naval patrol vessels built by Brodogradiliste '23 Maj' at Rijeka in 1952. Josef Broz Tito, the Croat resistance leader who became

consequently abandoned in Monte Carlo. After the public auction she ended up at the Valdetarro Shipyard in La Spezia. At the time this yard was busy building six 34m (112ft) steel sailing yachts (see *Runaway* in Refit 2001) to a Laurent Giles design and so the same naval architects were asked to prepare plans for a complete refit of *Istranka*. This they did with utmost thoroughness, preparing no fewer than 1,000 drawings. Work began in 1990 in a dry dock, which was especially built around *Istranka*. She was completely stripped to bare metal and major repairs were made to the structure including extensive replating below the waterline. Virtually all her equipment was junked and new main engines and generators were ordered.

At this stage the sailing yacht contract, which depended on the French 'defiscalization' programme, went badly wrong and the Valdetarro shipyard was forced to close. Work on *Istranka* stopped immediately and she sat quietly gathering dust in her covered dry dock for the next four years. Her saviours were a local firm of shipping agents and brokers named EEC Shipping who found a buyer who had been looking for a classic yacht and secured the finances to complete the refit. They rented the necessary space at the former Valdetarro yard and employed some of the engineers and craftsmen who had worked on her before. In addition, Ing. Guiseppe Sole was retained as interior designer while some well-known companies such

**Below:** doors to port and starboard of the wheelhouse provide access to the upper deck. Here a large table and director chairs enable up to 12 guests to dine in comfort

President of the new state of Yugoslavia, decided that the country should have a presidential yacht and *Istranka* was built on this existing hull design. It was a good choice as she ended up looking rather like a pre-Second World War Camper & Nicholsons motor yacht with a raised foredeck, knuckled bow and pretty counter stern.

Tito loved the yacht and used her frequently to carry favoured guests to his private island of Brioni, in the northern Adriatic. Newsreels from that time show him chatting with political heavyweights such as Nikita Khrushchev aboard *Istranka*. This favoured existence came to an end in 1976 when Tito died, after which *Istranka* was sold. Lacking essential maintenance, she was not a success as a charter yacht and went steadily downhill until, with a mounting pile of unpaid bills, her owners went bankrupt and she was

as Arredamenti Porto and Cantiere Navale Istria came on board as subcontractors.

Despite the fact that *Istranka* is a period yacht, an early decision was taken to use only top quality new equipment and materials. In fact, almost the only original piece of machinery on board is the anchor windlass which was considered worth refurbishing because it looks right.

A big problem was restarting work that had begun a decade before. The Deutz main engines, for instance, had never been run but were 10 years old. Their installation was a challenge because *Istranka*'s engine room is in the traditional position amidships, driving twin screws via quite long shafts running under the aft accommodation. Noise and vibration can always be a problem with this layout so it was particularly satisfying when she turned out to be very quiet, thanks to great care being taken with alignment and to the smooth-running five-bladed Finnscrew propellers. There is full computer monitoring of the main engines and other major systems.

Compared to a modern yacht, *Istranka* is fairly narrow and does not have a complete upper deck, so the volume of her accommodation is roughly what one would expect to find on a 35m (115ft) yacht built today. On the other hand she has much more character than a modern yacht, including sheered and cambered decks. The long, gently-curved side decks with teak-panelled bulwarks give a particularly ship-like feel but at the same time result in a fairly narrow main saloon.

*Istranka* has three levels of deck, beginning with a small sun deck on top of the superstructure with a semicircular seat around the funnel and two cushioned areas. The most attractive deck is one level down where a broad area of laid teak deck, which uses the full beam of the vessel, stretches back from the funnel to the aft end of the superstructure. A permanent awning on a stainless steel frame covers roughly half this deck and has sides with plastic windows that can be rolled down in bad weather. This semi-enclosed deck goes a long way towards making up for the lack of an upper saloon and is the ideal place for alfresco dining at the oval teak table surrounded by yellow and white upholstered director chairs.

In order to make best use of what was originally the boat deck, the two tenders have been moved to the foredeck where there is just enough room

**Top:** the renewal of work on the engine room that had actually been started 10 years previously proved particularly challenging

**Above:** craftsmen carry out their meticulous work

**Right:** *Istranka* laid up in the former Valdetarro Shipyard

for them along with a jet-ski with a centrally-placed launching crane. While convenient for cruising, it might be necessary to move the boats aft for serious passage-making.

At main deck level there is another smaller deck on the tapering stern and this also has a permanent awning over it. The relatively small area is utilized as fully as possible, having a circular breakfast table and four comfortable chairs, while the deck lockers have been given cushions to turn them into impromptu settees.

Careful planning was needed to make the best use of the rather narrow main saloon, the solution being to fit settees along one side only and bookshelves and a comprehensive entertainment centre along the other. A pair of glass-topped coffee tables are offset to starboard, leaving room to pass through without walking down the middle of the seating area. Far from being heavy and traditional, the decor is light, bright and modern, with limed oak woodwork providing a neutral background for the blue settees and bright scarlet leather tub chairs by Fran. The deck is polished teak with a large Persian rug under the furniture.

The forward end of the saloon is occupied by an oval table and eight Chiavarine chairs, standing on another oriental rug. Both the saloon and dining areas have panels of twinkling fibre-optic lights above them. A feature of the interior is the collection of prints of impressionist paintings found

in most compartments. For instance a pair of Van Goghs add life and colour to the dining area.

From the port side of the dining room a corridor runs forward to a hallway where there are stairs leading up to the bridge, and then continues on to the owner's accommodation which uses the full

**Above and top:** the foredeck was completely reconstructed to accommodate the two tenders, a 6m (20ft) Vetus Bellus and a Novamarine 450 Jet

beam of the hull beneath the raised foredeck. The first compartment is the owner's studio, which is virtually a second saloon with a comfortable sofa and coffee table as well as a breakfast table with two chairs. A plasma screen television has a connection to the satellite receiver while the telephone has private access to the Inmarsat system. A rather special feature is a watertight door opening directly onto the port side deck, giving a pleasing view along the whole length of the vessel towards the stern.

The owner's stateroom is large and comfortable, with a central double bed. However there is still plenty of space remaining for a dressing table and walk-in wardrobe. Opposite the bed, doors open on either side of a life-size reproduction of a painting by Gabrielle Dante Rossetti into twin marble-floored bathrooms which share a central shower.

The three guest cabins are on the lower deck aft and consist of two large doubles and a twin with traditional fitted bunks in the tapered part of the stern. All three have en suite bathrooms and are built to the same standard of

**Far left:** *Istranka's* narrow beam meant that careful planning had to be given to the dining and saloon areas to optimize the use of space (below left)

**Left:** forward of the main deck is the impressively large owner's stateroom, boasting a central king-sized bed

**Below:** the owner's stateroom was completely stripped back during its refurbishment

comfort with excellent woodwork and a good entertainment centre.

The whole of the lower deck forward of the engine room is devoted to the crew as well as a very well designed stainless steel galley with a full outfit of professional catering equipment. Eight crew are accommodated in four twin cabins with en suite showers, while the captain has a private cabin abaft the bridge. Also on the lower deck are freezers, cold rooms, dry storage and a fully-equipped laundry.

The teak-decked and panelled bridge is an intriguing mixture of classic and modern. The upright windows, with spinning clear-view screens, and the teak steering wheel seem traditional but all the equipment is entirely up-to-date, including twin radars, electronic chart system, full computer monitoring and a complete outfit of satellite communications equipment.

Classic yachts are often more attractive and interesting than modern yachts, but tired structures, old equipment and worn-out machinery are nothing but a headache for both owners and crew. *Istranka* is a historic and characterful ship which has been rebuilt as a completely new vessel with no old or troublesome features remaining. For an owner who has a great appreciation for a classic appearance and an interesting history, she does undoubtedly offer the best of the old and the new.

## SPECIFICATIONS

**LOA**
45.65m (149ft 8in)

**BEAM**
7.60m (24ft 11in)

**DRAUGHT**
3.13m (10ft 4in)

**GROSS TONNAGE**
341 tonnes

**PROPULSION**
2 x Deutz MWM TBD 440-6,
900hp

**GENERATORS**
2 x Deutz MWM 75kW
1 Cummins 45kW

**SPEED (MAX)**
16 knots

**RANGE @ 14 KNOTS**
4,500nm

**CLASSIFICATION**
Lloyds ✠100 A1

**BUILDER**
Brodogradiliste '23 Maj'
Rijeka/1952

**REFIT NAVAL ARCHITECTS**
Laurent Giles & Partners

**INTERIOR DESIGN**
Ing. Guiseppe Sole

**REFITTED BY**
Former 'Valdetarro Shipyard'
coordinated by EEC Shipping/2000

**PRINCIPAL EQUIPMENT**
Air-conditioning: Condaria
Stablilizers: Vosper
Watermakers: Idromar
Sewage treatment: Hamman
Propellers: Finnscrew
Engine controls: Mannesmann
Monitoring system: S Giorgio
SEIN
Boat crane: Sanguinetti
Satellite TV: Seatel
Satcom M: Magnavox
Satcom C: Sailor; Navtex: JRC
Radars: Decca Racal & JRC
GPS: JRC
Giro compass and autopilot:
Litton Plath

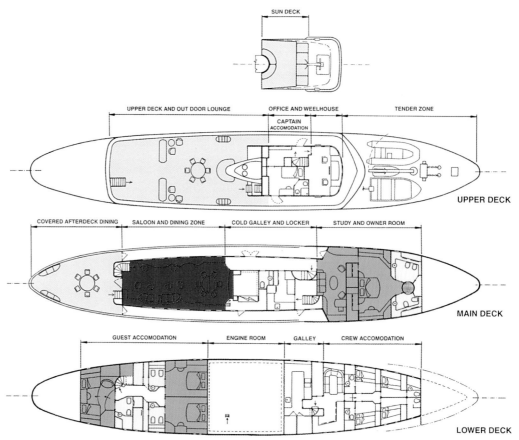

# INTERIORS

## EXCLUSIVE INTERIORS FOR THE FINEST LUXURY YACHTS

Loher, a family business founded in 1931 prides itself on providing a first class turn-key service from initial concept through manufacture and final installation.

Highest quality materials, creative schemes and skills craftsmanship are combined to produce furniture both individual in concept and exclusive in design.

**LOHER RAUMEXCLUSIV GMBH**
**WALLERSDORFER STRASSE 17 • 94522 WALLERSDORF - HAIDLFLING • GERMANY**
**PHONE +49 - (0) 99 33 - 910 - 105 • +49 - (0) 99 33 - 910-0**
**FAX +49 - (0) 99 33 - 910 - 280**
**e-mail: info@loher-raumexclusiv.de • www.loher-raumexclusiv.de**

# Magistral

**Below:** as *Orejona*, *Magistral*'s sail area was rather small for her size and is now 25 per cent larger

The extraordinary bond of affection that grows up between owners and their yachts should never be underestimated. Once forged it is difficult indeed to break and can often lead to sums of money being spent on a vessel that would be hard to justify on purely rational grounds. The schooner *Orejona* was not in bad condition at all considering her 27 years of service, but has now been relaunched as the totally renewed *Magistral* following a rebuilding programme that took two years to complete.

*Orejona* was not constructed for her present owner but he had cruised in her for seven very enjoyable years before deciding that she needed a limited refit as she had not received major attention for 15 years. The design by W de Vries Lentsch was very fine but had certain shortcomings. Among these was the fact that she lacked a really useful deck saloon. Her wheelhouse stood aft of the main mast and separate from the companionway leading below. Attached to the rear of the wheelhouse was a strange little doghouse that looked like an afterthought. Her guest accommodation required modernizing and

her sail area needed to be increased to improve her performance in light winds.

While thinking about this, the owner had the opportunity to look over the 33m (108ft) sloop *Amadeus* which had recently been rebuilt by the JFA Shipyard at Concarneau (see *Refit Annual 2000*). Although a yacht of very different character, he liked the way *Amadeus* was arranged, especially aft where *Orejona* lacked easy access to the sea. As a result he contacted Frederic Jaouen of JFA who proposed adding 2m (7ft) to the length of *Orejona* with a remodelled stern, rebuilding the superstructure,

**Above:** with all sails set, *Magistral* shows off her new teak decks and royal blue Awlgrip-painted topsides

modernizing the guest accommodation and improving the rig.

This plan was accepted and *Orejona* sailed into Concarneau in June 1999. However soon after work had begun to remove the old wheelhouse, the owner had a sudden change of heart. Instead of this limited but still quite extensive refit, he decided on a total rebuild. The old plan was torn up and JFA was instructed to strip her out completely. They took out literally every single thing that could be removed including the teak deck, the superstructure, the rig, the entire contents of the

engine room, all of the wiring, plumbing, woodwork and furniture, until nothing was left but a bare steel hull which was then sand-blasted to bright metal inside and out.

After that, they began to build a new vessel which was no longer to be named *Orejona* but *Magistral* in recognition of her new identity. The condition of the hull, solidly built by the Dutch shipyard Cammenga in 1972, was excellent and only needed minor repairs and attention to tank-tops before new work could begin.

The owner decided to commission Andrew Winch

**Above:** the extended stern was built in steel, adding 2m (7ft) to the yacht's overall length

**Below:** re-teaking the foredeck

**Bottom:** all the old pipework was ripped out and replaced

to design a new interior that would be comfortable, fairly traditional and very appealing to look at. Meanwhile JFA called in Berret Racoupeau of La Rochelle to design the extended stern and new superstructure. Altering another designer's hull lines can be tricky but in fact *Orejona*'s transom stern had been a bit brutal and the extended counter designed by Berret is a definite improvement and a better match for the handsome clipper bow.

The new stern was built while the hull was completely empty, so there was no damage to existing services or accommodation. Although only 2m (7ft) was added to the vessel's overall length, it provides many of the features that *Orejona* lacked. To maximize the space, the deck was raised above the new section without increasing the height of the original bulwark line. A teak-planked transom door hinges down to form a boarding platform from which a stairway leads up to the deck. Offset to one side is a an extending passerelle for Mediterranean berthing while the large lazarette has space for an inflatable dinghy or jet-ski and other sports equipment.

Not a centimetre of the stern extension is wasted; under the floor is a new tank carrying five additional tons of fuel while on deck is a new outside steering position and instrument console.

The new, completely integrated superstructure

has made a dramatic improvement to the accommodation. From aft, one enters the cockpit, which is protected by a roof, but has open sides. It boasts comfortable L-shaped settees on either side with a pair of teak tables which can be joined together with hinged flaps to create a large alfresco dining area. Through double doors one then reaches the deck saloon which is completely enclosed but has large windows all around it. To starboard is a comfortable seating area and table; to port a cosy bar in front of which is the inside steering position and navigation desk. Even the roof is put to use: a low rail makes it possible to place cushions there and use it as a sunbathing area.

Steps lead down to the main saloon and dining area which adopts more-or-less the old layout, but is just completely refurbished. The large, square windows provide plenty of natural light and prevent the impression of being 'below decks' which so often makes people feel uncomfortable on sailing yachts. Being in the widest part of this beamy hull means that there is plenty of room for seating and tables on each side of this relaxing compartment. The really clever feature of this interior design was to open up the main saloon so that it became part of a much larger compartment on two levels. The original saloon was reached via a steep companionway ladder, giving a somewhat claustrophobic atmosphere, whereas in the new saloon, a broad, open stairway leads up to the deck saloon or down to the guest cabins, while the mizzen mast acts as an eye-catching central feature.

The owner and guest accommodation, which uses the whole of the area aft of the saloon, has been replanned to make better use of space and increase the capacity from six to eight people. In place of the old full-width owner's stateroom, there are now two en suite double guest cabins of identical size. The owner's stateroom is forward on the port side of the offset corridor with an enlarged bathroom that includes a proper tub. Finally, on the opposite side of the corridor is a smaller twin cabin with en suite shower room. The whole guest area has been beautifully fitted out in teak, completed to a very high standard in JFA's own modern joinery and finishing workshops. For this classic Dutch ship the yard has aimed for the best Dutch standard of finish and has undoubtedly achieved it.

*Magistral* is planned in the first instance as a private yacht, but the revised accommodation makes her much more suitable for charter use if required.

The owner was very keen to retain his loyal crew of six (the captain has monitored every detail of the two-year rebuild) and insisted that their quarters should provide a comfortable long-term home-from-home. The captain's cabin, for instance, has its own small lounge/office and generous shower room while both the other crew cabins have en suite shower rooms. Crew become frustrated if they do not have sufficient space to work but

*Magistral* has a well-planned galley and separate laundry in addition to a proper crew mess, all beautifully finished in mahogany.

A new, much improved access from the crew's quarters to the deck means that the crew avoid having to keep walking through the main saloon which is never popular with them or guests.

Of the engine room it is almost sufficient to say that every single piece of equipment in it is new and that, except for the 600hp MAN main engine, there are two of nearly everything – two generators, two air-conditioning units, two watermakers and so forth. A special feature is that every piece of equipment that can drip is mounted in a stainless-steel drip tray so that *Magistral*'s bilges should remain as spotlessly clean as they are now. With the addition of the new aft tank, a total of 24 tons of fuel can be carried, easily sufficient to give transatlantic range under power.

The old photograph of *Orejona* shows that her sailplan was a bit too small for her size and considerable weight. The owner was keen to keep the original masts but these have been completely refurbished and re-rigged.

The extended stern made it possible to fit a considerably longer mizzen boom, resulting in a much larger and better shaped sail with conventional rather than roller furling. By raising the mizzen forestay to the masthead, the staysail and fisherman are both increased in area.

The working sail area is now 25 per cent larger than before and, just for fun, there is a 400m²

**Below:** the old wheelhouse was removed and a completely new deck saloon built in its place

**Below right and bottom:** the main saloon and dining area retains the original layout, but the fact that it is now open to the deck saloon creates a completely different atmosphere

**Far right:** the owner's stateroom, adjoined to a spacious bathroom, is superbly finished in teak. The former full-width owner's stateroom, sporting a marine-patterned fabric, was located towards the stern and has now been replaced by two double guest cabins

(4,304sqft) spinnaker in the locker. A complete outfit of Lewmar powered winches will make it relatively easy for the crew to handle this increased sail area. With a displacement of 180 tons and a fixed propeller, *Magistral* is never going to be a racer, but in trials everyone was very impressed by her performance under the new rig.

On deck, as below, virtually everything, including the deck itself, is new. One exception is the massive anchor windlass which has been retained because it looks right. Together with the brass bell it gives

the proper feeling of being aboard a real ship.

Lying alongside JFA's pontoon at Concarneau, with her new teak decks gleaming and new royal blue Awlgrip paint reflecting the Spring sunshine, *Magistral* looked extremely smart and impatient to begin sailing. It was very noticeable that the small addition in overall length, combined with the dark colour scheme, makes her appear considerably longer and more elegant than she did previously. She was a fine yacht before, but she is a magnificent one now.

## SPECIFICATIONS

| | |
|---|---|
| **LOA** | 36.3m (119ft 1in) |
| **BEAM** | 8.0m (26ft 3in) |
| **DRAUGHT** | 3.5m (11ft 6in) |
| **DISPLACEMENT (LIGHT)** | 180 tons |
| **SAIL AREA (WORKING)** | 526m² (5,662sqft) |
| **CONSTRUCTION** | Welded steel |
| **PROPULSION** | MAN 2840, 600hp |
| **GENERATORS** | 2 x Onan 56kVa |
| **SPEED UNDER POWER** | 11.8 knots |
| **RANGE @ 9 KNOTS** | 3,500nm |
| **FUEL CAPACITY** | 24,000 litres |
| **FRESH WATER CAPACITY** | 2,000 litres |
| **NAVAL ARCHITECT** | W De Vries Lentsch |
| **BUILDER** | Cammenga/1972 |
| **REFIT NAVAL ARCHITECT** | Berret Racoupeau |
| **REFIT INTERIOR DESIGN** | Andrew Winch Design |
| **REFIT YARD/2001** | Chantier Naval JFA<br>Quai du Moros<br>Rive Gauche<br>29900 Concarneau, France<br>Tel:+33 2 98 60 49 48<br>Fax:+33 2 98 60 49 40<br>Email: jfa.cn@wanadoo.fr |

**PRINCIPAL EQUIPMENT**
Gearbox: ZF BW190 with PTO
Propeller: Helicia 4 blade
Masts: John Powell Masts
Boom: Sparcraft
Rigging: Navtec
Sails: Incidence

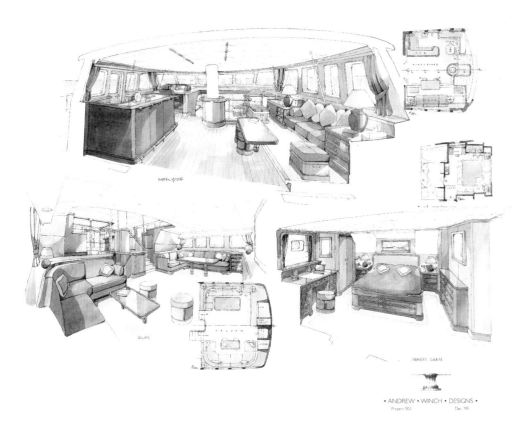

• ANDREW • WINCH • DESIGNS •
Project 501          Dec '99

# Chantier Naval JFA

Thanks to a major investment programme in recent years, JFA has excellent facilities for both refit and new building at Concarneau in Britanny, Northern France, and is able to work on yachts up to 45m (148ft) in length under cover. The yard is equipped to deal with wood, metal or plastics and has its own modern mechanical, electrical and joinery workshops as well as several paint-spraying cabins.

Alongside the yard there is a boat lift with a capacity of 2,000 tonnes from which vessels can be moved directly into JFA's shed. In front of the yard there is a serviced quay of 100m (328ft) in length and 6m (20ft) in depth along with a pontoon where fitting out work is completed.

The company's intention is always to have one major refit in progress plus one or two new building projects at the same time, as this allows it to use its facilities and workforce to the best advantage. This year the yard will complete a high performance aluminium cruiser-racer and begin work building a new 37m (122ft) 'Expedition yacht' to a Vripack design.

*Magistral* was its second major refit of a sailing yacht, the first being the 33m (108ft) cutter *Amadeus* (see *Refit Annual 2000*).

Concarneau, with its ancient walled citadel, set in the delightful Baie de la Foret, is well worth a visit in its own right. It is in the centre of the prettiest part of the Brittany coast, close to the anchorages of Benodet and Loctudy. A short distance offshore lie the Iles de Glenan, home of the famous sea school that has introduced thousands of people to sailing. The area is easy to reach with daily flights from Paris to the airports of Quimper, Concarneau or Brest.

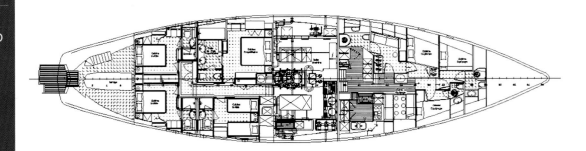

# JFA Chantier Naval

You are demanding,
We are passionate...

Magistral 118'

Vripack 122'

**W**e like to use all types of materials and construction techniques for one-of-a-kind boats. This also applies when restoring sailing yachts and motor yachts from 75' to 150'. We have the ideal infrastructure (2000 ton lift, 330 foot launching dock with 20 ft depth, new bays and workshops) and above all experienced craftsmen, capable of the most beautiful realizations. We are not satisfied with just making good-looking boats, but also to build them according to the rules of the art with the highest quality workmanship as well as using beautiful and durable materials… for your greatest pleasure and pride.

**JFA** - Quai des Seychelles - 29900 Concarneau - France - Tel : 33 0 2 98 60 49 48 - Fax : 33 0 2 98 60 49 40 - E-mail : jfa.cn@wanadoo.fr - Internet : jfa-yachts.com

# Moonraker

**Right:** launched originally for an owner with an obsession for speed, the aim of *Moonraker*'s refit was to improve all aspects of her comfort and style, while still retaining her essential quality as a high performance superyacht

**Below:** built at Norship International in 1992, *Moonraker* made history by setting a new world speed record for a yacht over 30m (100ft), reaching in excess of 66 knots

Old racehorses are put out to pasture, vintage Grand Prix cars end up in motor museums, and retired Olympic medallists become spokesmen and women for cereals. But what happens to record-breaking yachts after their prime?

In the case of *Moonraker*, a refit lasting two years and costing US$6 million not only freshened up the interior and styling of the yacht, but gave her a whole new lease of life. She was a challenge to build and just as much a challenge to refit.

*Moonraker* was originally constructed for John Staluppi, an American car dealer with a penchant for speed. After a series of smaller performance boats, Staluppi commissioned *For Your Eyes Only*, a 30.5m (100ft) Denison with water jet propulsion and a speed of 34 knots that essentially marked the beginning of the new era of high-speed superyachts. Staluppi soon launched a 40.2m (132ft) Diaship which, to carry on the James Bond theme, he named *Octopussy*. This boat went on to set a superyacht speed record, attaining 53 knots.

Still not content, Staluppi gave Frank Mulder the task of designing a truly fast yacht, which resulted in the 35.36m (116ft) *Moonraker* from Norship International. Up to that time, Norship had specialized in high-speed catamaran ferries and surface-effect minesweepers for various navies, which gave them the expertise to build such a demanding vessel. While Mulder had designed *Moonraker* for aluminium

construction, Staluppi decided to switch to composites when he saw that the weight savings could help in his search for speed.

The technical challenge for Norship was to build composite panels able to withstand the loads generated at more than 60 knots. Using a sandwich of E-glass and Divinycel foam coring with DNV approvals, *Moonraker* combined sleek good looks with the lowest structural weight that could be achieved at the time. Much of the joinery was created from thin wood veneers on honeycomb cores, and even the marble flooring was cut to cardboard-thin sheets and bonded to low-density boards to save weight.

In addition to the lightweight construction, *Moonraker* also had ample power in the form of twin MTU 16-cylinder diesels, totalling 6,960hp, as well as a Textron Lycoming gas turbine of 4,600hp. With nearly 12,000hp blasting through huge KaMeWa water jets, *Moonraker* easily set a new world superyacht speed record of more than 66 knots or 75mph.

Seven years later, Staluppi had moved on to other projects and *Moonraker* was ready for attention. The turbine had long since been removed, although the twin MTUs provided sufficient power to still make her

a very fast yacht capable of over 35 knots. But there had been trade-offs made in the original pursuit for speed and it was time to rectify them.

The decision was taken by the owner and Captain Matt Ploof to contract the refit project themselves. Rather than simply delivering the yacht to one yard to handle the diverse project, they would pick and choose from specialists who would be responsible for their areas of expertise.

The starting point was to take the yacht to the Derecktor yard in Fort Lauderdale, where Consolidated Yacht Corporation was leasing a shed for its operation. Experts in engineering and composite construction, Consolidated was given the task of extending the sun deck, which had been truncated originally in the quest for light weight. The small sun deck was adequate at 66 knots, but cramped in comparison to similar 35m (115ft) yachts. The original design for the extension had been to utilize support posts from the aft deck, however the owner was adamant that he wanted to find a way to suspend the sun deck without posts. Consolidated built the sun deck extension with the latest composite technology, utilizing carbon-fibre and Kevlar not

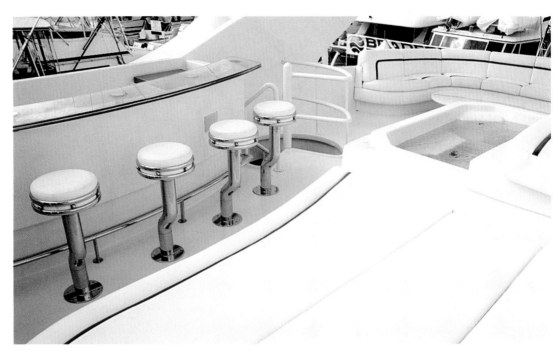

**Right:** the new sun deck comes complete with a six-person sunpad that conceals a spa pool, as well as a spacious bar

**Below right:** all the anchor gear, including the windlass, warping capstans and even the hawse eyes and cleats, have been upgraded

**Far right:** Art-line produced the original modern-looking interior, which at the time was appropriate for the world's fastest superyacht. Now, however, the accommodation, designed by JC Espinosa, has adopted a more subtle tone, which is clearly exemplified in the main saloon where an unpatterned off-white Kalogridis wool and silk carpet enhances the feeling of space

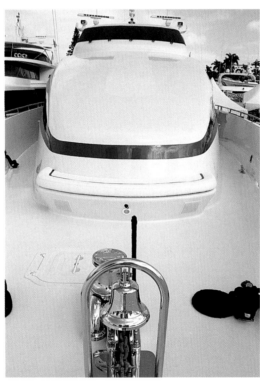

only for strength but to prevent any possibility of harmonic vibration from the unsupported deck.

While Consolidated was working on the exterior, *Moonraker* was literally gutted inside and JC Espinosa masterminded an all new interior design. Elegance In Wood of Destin, Florida, (now called Prestige Interiors), which specializes in luxury interiors for aircraft, recreational vehicles and yacht companies such as Destiny, provided all the new joinery and soft furnishings.

Next, *Moonraker* was towed to the Roscioli yard in Fort Lauderdale where, in a covered shed, the yacht was flawlessly repainted while the interior refurbishing continued unabated.

One of the trickiest parts of the refit, according to Captain Ploof, was coordinating as many as 50 different subcontractors so that each had the time and

space for their part of the project without crowding the other contractors. It became a bit of a juggling act, especially as the electricians were unable to install certain wiring until the plumbing crew had finished, and the plumbers in turn had to work around the air-conditioning team. 'The logistics' says Ploof, 'were unbelievably complicated, and had to be continually refined because the refit grew and changed as it progressed.' Ploof also credits his First Officer John Helfrich as being '(his) right arm' in keeping the project on track. 'John gave 110 per cent and was instrumental in assisting with project management and quality control.'

Ward's Marine Electric renewed all wiring and power distribution panels and added a paralleling system for the generators. Nortek Group upgraded and replaced both the communication and navigation systems, and Media Dimensions installed a sophisticated audio-visual system with touch screen controls and a large hidden projection screen which rolls down from the main saloon headliner. A myriad of other trades were involved throughout the refit, including Comfort Marine Air and Dupuy Marine Plumbing. Also, National Marine Suppliers provided invaluable local support for many aspects of the project.

Once finished at Roscioli, *Moonraker* moved to the Bradford yard, where the water jet propulsions system was overhauled and the bottom was painted.

While the biggest single external change was reconfiguring the sun deck, the refit also incorporated upgrading all the anchor gear, including windlass, warping capstans and even the hawse eyes and cleats. The Aqua Air air-conditioning system was extensively upgraded, with a separate zone to provide cool air to the dining area on the aft deck. A lube oil transfer system was inserted, a second Matrix watermaker was installed, and all safety and bilge equipment was either replaced or completely overhauled. Nautical Structures built a hydraulic passerelle as well as twin hydraulic garage doors for the SeaDoo transom garages. A hydraulic lift system for the tender in the centre garage was also added.

The new Espinosa interior is contemporary without being as loud as the original, with bird's-

**Right and below:** although the pilothouse is still reminiscent of the controls on a space craft, the spiral staircase leading up to it from the main saloon has been radically altered

**Far right:** the circular bed on a raised platform continues to be a prominent feature of the master stateroom. The décor, however, is more muted, contrasting with the sparkling mirrors and abundance of downlights which previously existed

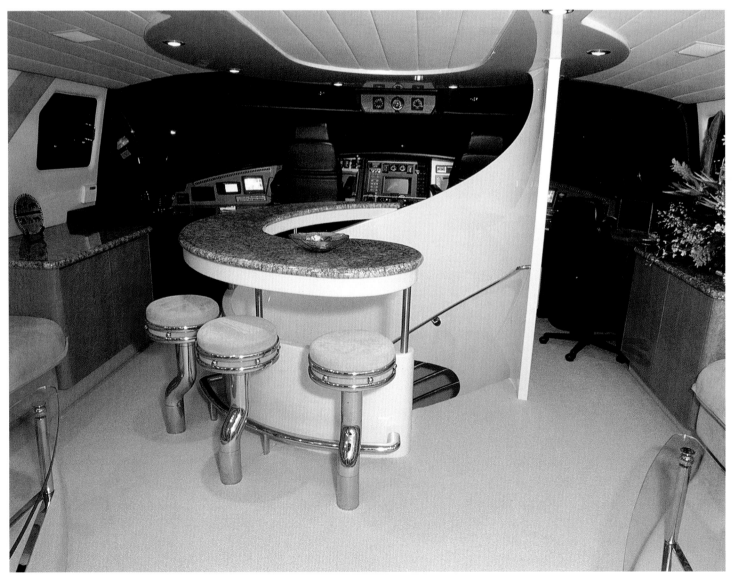

eye maple panelling, soft leather seating, and off-white Kalogridis wool and silk carpeting.

The saloon boasts a bar to port with a counter of crushed shells and travertine marble flooring. To starboard is a NovaSuede leather settee with pull-out foot-rests, and the six-tiered Malcolm Cole custom oval stainless steel balustrade accents the forward stairs leading up to the sky lounge or down to the guest quarters.

The midship galley, which had been one of the instigating factors in the refit, is completely new, facing the dining area which features a Chris Channell etched glass backlit wall sculpture of humpback whales. Both the breakfast bar, with an electric screen for privacy and five Malcolm Cole stools, and the dining table are made from marble.

The master suite, which once sported a gym area separated by a glass panel that could be turned opaque electrically, has been completely revamped. The circular bed remains, but the gym has been turned into a business-like office area. The stateroom itself features raw silk bedcovers, pillows of Shantung silk and Perlato marble counters. The master bathroom is divided by the central doorway,

**Right:** the engine room houses two
MTU diesels driving KaMeWa jet units

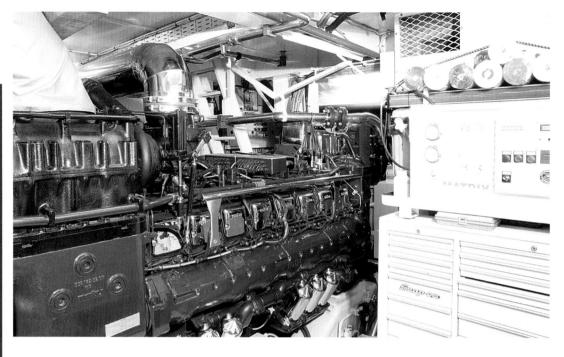

## SPECIFICATIONS

**LOA**
35.36m (116ft)

**BEAM**
7.14m (23ft 5in)

**DRAUGHT**
1.6m (5ft 2in)

**CONSTRUCTION**
Composite plastics

**PROPULSION**
2 x MTU 16V396TB94
(3,480hp ea)

**GENERATORS**
2 x Northern Lights 60kW

**FUEL**
8,600 US gallons (32,550 litres)

**WATER**
1,387 US gallons (5,250 litres)

**SPEED**
(max) 35 knots / (cruise) 28 knots

**NAVAL ARCHITECT**
Frank Mulder

**REFIT INTERIOR DESIGN**
JC Espinosa

**BUILDER**
Norship International

**REFIT**
Consolidated Yacht Corporation
Tel:+1 305 643 0334
Fax:+1 305 643 1897
Roscioli Yachting Center
Tel:+1 954 581 9200
Fax:+1 954 791 0958
Bradford Marine
Tel:+1 954 791 3800
Fax:+1 954 583 9938

**PRINCIPAL CONTRACTORS**
Joinery & soft furnishings:
Elegance In Wood
(Prestige Interiors)
Electrics: Ward's Marine
Plumbing: DuPuy Marine
Electronics: Nortek Group,
DMP America

and is equipped with a whirlpool tub, separate shower and travertine marble flooring.

The pilothouse still bears witness to *Moonraker*'s high-speed origin, resembling the control console on a space shuttle rather than a yacht. There are twin leather Recaro electrically-controlled and heated seats, with a joystick on the right arm of the captain's chair, while a large panel surrounding the ship's monitoring systems between the seats is finished in bird's-eye maple.

The sun deck extension completely covers the aft deck and, where it once had just a dinette, it now has a six-person sunpad with electric backrests and a spa pool hidden underneath, a wrap-around seat aft, and a spacious bar with five stools facing an underlit cracked glass counter. In addition to the Gaggenau electric grill, the bar features a double chamber frozen drinks machine.

While masterminding every facet of an extensive refit is not for everyone, *Moonraker* shows that it is possible and even advantageous to seek out the very best in each field and coordinate their efforts to achieve a finished yacht that is superior to what could have been created at a single yard.

With literally every system changed, upgraded or overhauled, *Moonraker* is no longer the lightweight racehorse that once set a world speed record, but has matured into a luxurious and well-fitted superyacht that still bears a proud name.

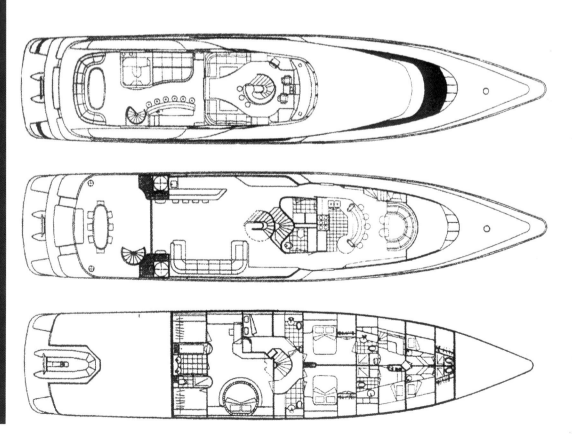

# Kaori

In her shining, smart, dark blue livery, with a sweeping sheer line, uncluttered decks and elegant deck saloon, *Kaori* immediately attracts the attention befitting a new yacht in every port she enters. In reality, however, it is the transformation from old to new that has given *Kaori* the new look and character she proudly exhibits today.

The story began in the Caribbean back in 1992, when a happy charter guest and his captain, Martin Lucas, sowed the seeds of a strong relationship, the benefits of which they would both be enjoying some nine years later. True to his word, the charter guest himself became a yacht owner in 1997 when he purchased the well-known Ron Holland 32.6m (107ft) *Shanakee* and duly asked Lucas to become his captain. Re-named *Nipara*, the yacht gave the owner some great cruising over the next two years, after which he sold her with a view to buying something larger.

This, however, proved to be easier said than done in a flourishing market, where new build lead times were at a minimum of two years. A broader perspective was called for, and it was with this in mind that the owner received a call from prolific yacht broker and friend Bill Sanderson, to join him over in Auckland to view the 38.1m (125ft) 1991-built Palmer Johnson schooner *Mandalay*, which was just about to be released onto the market. Suddenly, thoughts were turned to a whole new and exciting

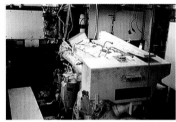

**Above right:** *Kaori's* rubbing strake came up well after 12 coats of varnish

**Top:** the masts were unstepped and taken back to Southern Spars to be reconditioned

**Centre and above:** out with the old and in with the new. Among the engine room's new equipment are two Northern Lights units and 3,000Ah of batteries and chargers

possibility; that of refitting a suitable in-commission vessel to produce a contemporary yacht with personal style, in the fraction of the time of a new build.

Three days later, Captain Martin Lucas was in Auckland and the venture was under way. Positive feedback from Lucas immediately saw his client making haste 'down under' and before long they were out on the water giving *Mandalay* a sea trial, while discussions ensued over what changes could be made, in line with the feasibility of the whole project.

Initial feelings confirmed the basic suitability of the vessel for the owner's requirements. At 38.1m (125ft), she was certainly large enough and had plenty of internal volume, though it was felt that the layout of the accommodation would require some changes in order to incorporate greater flexibility, and a major cosmetic upgrade was needed throughout.

Looking at her exterior, which was finished in white from the waterline to the top of the equipment mounted above her deck saloon, it was felt that she looked somewhat cumbersome, although not in an insurmountable way that some moderate structural changes up top and a complete repaint could not overcome. Finally, in order to achieve the first-class operational use requirements of the vessel, it became clear that she would need a comprehensive overhaul of all her mechanical, electrical, engineering and sailing systems, including her rig, with any replacements to be carried out as deemed necessary.

Time was very much of the essence. Auckland-based boatbuilder McMullen & Wing had both the space and an available workforce, and after a number of meetings with the yard as well as a multitude of external contractors, the owner gave Captain Lucas the go-ahead and a deadline. In just eight months, the yacht, now renamed *Kaori*, was to have been completely refitted and transported to the east coast of America.

Externally, it was decided that the object of improving *Kaori's* profile could be best achieved by removing the bulky fixed arch over the aft deck as well as clearing the contour of the deck saloon.

Besides applying a fresh coat of white Awlgrip to the coachroof and deck saloon, the topsides were repainted in a superb traditional dark navy blue, and with the provision of an attractive gold leaf cove stripe and a raised white waterline, these changes combined to give a greatly enhanced and pleasingly balanced profile.

The masts were removed and delivered to Southern Spars in Auckland, where the internal cabling and trunking were replaced and new spreader lights were fitted. They were then repainted with a white Awlgrip paint finish. On the main mast, a custom stainless steel bracket was built for the radar scanner, which was fitted along with two satcom Mini-M domes above the first spreaders.

Both booms were overhauled while all deck hydraulics and vang gears were removed and reconditioned. The standing rigging was also thoroughly inspected, with new terminals fitted where appropriate and all running rigging renewed. The original schooner sailing rig incorporated staysail and fisherman sails on the foremast, which were consequently changed to a single in-mast furling sail, giving Captain Lucas a much more manageable and effective set up. With a new suit of Doyle sails, the rig overhaul was complete.

Out on deck, all stainless steel stanchions, mooring cleats and car tracks were removed and machine polished to an exemplary standard. The pulpit stainless steel was reworked to incorporate two new navigation lights, while two new 400lb stainless steel CQR anchors completed the purposeful look at the bow. In addition, both windlasses were removed, stripped and rebuilt, as were all deck winches.

On the deck itself, every fitting was removed before it was sanded down in full and then totally recaulked, giving the teak a rewarding flush look and feel as a result. All deck hatches received the benefit of new Lexan glass, while the deck lockers themselves were the subject of a thorough overhaul. The beautiful teak capping rail was also stripped back to bare wood and long-boarded, prior to receiving 12 coats of varnish to give a delightfully deep and lasting traditional shine.

Now, the aft deck, with handcrafted and deeply varnished teak, is a wonderful open relaxation area where guests spend the majority of their time. There are two new teak deck tables, incorporating retractable

**Above and left:** although the main saloon retains the same layout as before, the subtle beige shades chosen by the owner's wife create a relaxing environment

stands, and an additional centrepiece, allowing superb flexibility by joining the two tables together to seat up to 14 guests in comfort. The soft furnishings are in blue and white, and there are two beautiful, new custom teak steering wheels.

The two helm stations themselves now include twin bowthruster controls, VHF, B&G instrumentation and a daylight screen displaying the Transas electronic navigation package or the Vessel Information System.

Stepping into *Kaori*'s delightful open deck saloon, one is immediately taken by the easy-going atmosphere provided by the natural colours of the soft furnishings, chosen by the owner's wife, that extend throughout the interior. At the after end, the main mast section is veneered in teak – aft of which, a cabinet with a hydraulically retractable new 25-inch flat screen television monitor is integrated with both the yacht's navigation and entertainment sytems to allow maximum flexibility for guests and crew alike. At the forward end of the deck saloon, the pilothouse and

**Above and right:** the owner's stateroom has been refurbished in a rich, traditional style, with the use of light colours creating a sophisticated and comfortable look. It was previously dominated by a striking four-poster bed

electronic navigation and monitoring systems are mounted in a blue leather console.

Below, in the main saloon, the entertainment systems now include a 300 CD integrated sound system, allowing individual use from any of the multi-user stations situated throughout the yacht. A new 42-inch Panasonic plasma flat screen for television, DVD and VHS is hidden behind a removable false

bookcase containing gold leaf leather bound bookends.

The owner's original aim to increase the flexibility of the accommodation was inventively met by Captain Lucas and his team in three areas. Firstly, the sofa in the owner's study was converted so that it can become a pull-out athwartships double. Then, in the guest cabins, the addition of a beautifully blending pullman berth into the fore/aft bulkhead of one was

**Above and left:** one of the two guest cabins, where large twin beds have been converted into a double and a single. The blue and white upholstery creates a more nautical feel

further complemented by the conversion of two large singles into a double and single in the other.

In the engine room are two new Northern Lights generators. Other new equipment includes a Hamann waste treatment plant, an Alfa Laval fuel treatment unit, 3,000Ah of batteries and chargers and a custom electrical control panel for the engine room systems.

Today, *Kaori* has a new lease of life and, remarkably,

the huge number and scale of improvements were completed on time by the dedicated workforce at McMullen & Wing. One cannot help but feel that the largest factor behind the success of this refit emanates from the skills, knowledge and commitment of a first-rate professional captain, and also from an excellent owner/captain relationship, now amply rewarded by the triumphant result: *Kaori*.

## SPECIFICATIONS

**LOA**
38.1m (125ft)

**BEAM**
8.6m (28ft 2in)

**DRAUGHT**
3.1m (10ft)

**DISPLACEMENT**
179 tonnes

**FUEL CAPACITY**
21,764 litres

**FRESH WATER CAPACITY**
7,570 litres

**ELECTRONICS**
B&G Hydra, Transas electronic
charting

**SAILS**
Doyle

**ENGINES**
2 x CAT 3406 TA 312hp

**GENERATORS**
Northern Lights,
40 and 55kva

**NAVAL ARCHITECTURE**
Ernest Brierley, Chuck Paine
and Associates

**ORIGINAL INTERIOR
DESIGN**
Jane Plachter

**REFIT INTERIOR DESIGN**
Owner's wife and Captain
Martin Lucas

**BUILDER/YEAR**
Palmer Johnson/1991

**REFIT**
McMullen and Wing
27 Gabador Place
Mount Wellington
PO Box 14-218, Auckland
1006, New Zealand
Tel:+64 9 573 1405
Fax:+64 9 573 0393

# McMullen & Wing

Established in 1969, McMullen & Wing was a pioneer of aluminium yacht construction in New Zealand, building small racing sailboats in its Auckland boatyard. Later, its business expanded and diversified, with the construction of a range of aluminium pilot vessels and a series of steel-hulled motor sailers as well as several aluminium hulled launches with composite superstructures for the Auckland Police. In 1985, the company won the contract to build the composite-hulled 12-Metres, *Black Magic I* and *Black Magic II*, for the 1987 New Zealand America's Cup challenge, an event which set the pace for New Zealand's capture of the Cup two challenges later. In 1986, the company was purchased by David & Terry Porter, the present owners, who gradually changed its direction from building mid-sized sailing yachts towards the refit, rebuilding and more recently, the construction of superyachts, large sport fishing yachts and custom-designed high performance rigid inflatables (RIBs). The

list of famous yachts refitted includes names such as the Bruce King-designed ketch *Hetairos* and the 35.6m (117ft) Bill Dixon schooner *Yanneke-Too*. However, to date, its proudest achievement is without doubt the rebuild of the beautiful 54m (177ft) gaff-rigged schooner, *Shenandoah of Sark*.

Currently, the yard employs a skilled workforce of 125 and is working on *Surprise*, a 35m (115ft) steel-hulled expedition yacht from the board of the Setzer Design Group, its biggest new-build project to date, a 39.6m (130ft), 24-knot sportfisherman style motor yacht *Mea Culpa*, four further composite sport fishing yachts between 21.9m and 23.7m (72ft-78ft) and *Ipanema*, a 34.1m (112ft) German Frers sailing yacht being constructed from Alustar aluminium. Its facilities include nine dedicated operational areas in five buildings totalling an area of 9,290m² (100,000sqft), a 65-tonne travel lift and a 300-tonne slipway.

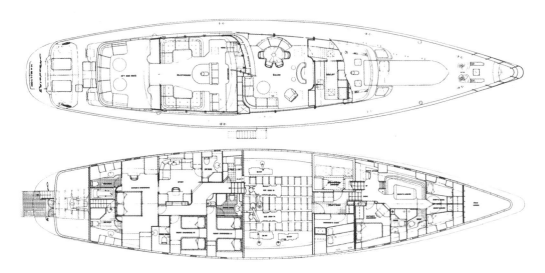

# Elenesse II

The modern superyacht is a very complex piece of machinery that needs to be properly maintained at all times. Without thorough care it can go downhill frighteningly quickly; the 42m (137ft 10in) motor yacht *Elenesse II* is a good example of how things can go wrong and the intense effort required to put them right again.

Launched in 1991 as *Antares I*, her welded steel hull was built by Benetti at Viareggio and completed by Mondo Marine at Genoa. Although not previously well-known in the yacht industry, Mondo is a large industrial group of which the Marsic Shipyard, close to Genoa Airport, is a part. The yard specializes in refit and repair while new building is carried out at the company's second yard at Savona, a few kilometres down the coast. *Antares I* was owned by a group of investors who took advantage of the now notorious 'Defiscalization' programme instituted by the French Government. Under its provisions, it was possible to build a vessel without paying the TVA tax (British VAT) provided she then plied for charter in French overseas waters for at least three years. It appeared very attractive to owners who could then sell at a useful profit without paying tax. The fatal flaws were firstly that the owners were normally anonymous 'investors' who had no knowledge of yachts, and secondly that the crew had to be drawn from the French merchant marine. Like the owners, they had no real interest in yachts and simply ran them like ferry-boats.

After three years of use in the Caribbean, during which seemingly no money or effort was devoted to maintenance, *Antares I* came back to the Mediterranean where she did some charters while looking for a buyer. By then she was starting to look scruffy and, failing to find a buyer, was laid up, first in Cannes and later in Toulon. Her price went down with the passing of time until eventually she represented an interesting opportunity to purchase and rebuild. A British businessman, who already owned a large motor yacht, asked surveyor Bernard Sivell-Muller to look her over and subsequently made an offer which was accepted in October 1999.

Sivell-Muller was then requested to act as project manager for a complete restoration to 'as new'

**Left:** after a 20-month refit at Marsic Shipyard in Italy, *Elenesse II* is now to all intents and purposes a brand new boat, being fully MCA compliant and having the capacity to accommodate up to 10 guests in the height of luxury

**Above:** As *Antares I*, *Elenesse II* chartered in Caribbean waters for three years, following her launch in 1991

**Top:** the stern was significantly extended by 3m (9ft 10in) in order to provide a bathing platform

**Above right:** replacing the bowthruster was tricky due to the complex curvature of the bulbous bow

**Above:** the engines had to be hoisted up to main deck level before being lifted away by a crane

standard and a contract was negotiated for the job to be done by her original builders Mondo Marine. Late in 1999, *Antares I* made it to Genoa, but only just, with one engine running and almost everything in the engine room leaking copiously. Here she was slipped and given a full ABS hull survey; the starting point for a rebuild of almost unbelievable thoroughness.

In addition to Sivell-Muller, the local consultant Sydac was retained as naval architect while class supervision remained with ABS. Registration is in the British Cayman Islands which, as a 'Red Ensign' state is able to issue MCA certification. This particular piece of paper is, of course, crucial for a

Red Ensign vessel that wishes to charter. Titan, Hyde & Torrance Brokers of Athens and London were engaged to handle her sale.

The hull condition was not bad, but the bowthruster needed replacing and this called for some tricky replating as the bulbous bow results in a complex shape in this area. Other hull repairs were minor but the real horrors were inside. Like most steel yachts she has double-bottom tanks and some of the tank-tops were found to be severely corroded. Worst of all was the black-water tank under the forward guest accommodation which had actually perforated, allowing the contents to slop out into the crew bilge. Repairing tank-tops is always tricky as the accommodation has to be completely dismantled to provide access, and in this case the working conditions could hardly have been more disagreeable.

The engine room turned out to be another disaster area. The condition of the equipment was such that the new owner decided to make a clean sweep and renew all the machinery including the two propulsion engines. Of course main engines are normally fitted at an early stage of construction and then entombed when the main deck is constructed above. To get them out called for the dining room to be dismantled and a large hole cut in the floor, above which a steel lifting frame was fitted. This enabled the engines, as well as other machinery, to be hoisted up to main deck level, placed on skids and dragged out through the saloon onto the aft deck from where they could be lifted away by crane. All the new machinery followed the same route in reverse.

In addition to two new Caterpillar main engines, the engine room swallowed up two new Kohler generators, new watermakers, air-conditioning sets, domestic hot-water boilers, redesigned exhaust systems, propeller shafts, steering gear, pipework, hydraulic lines, pumps and dials, fuel lines, electric switchboards and wiring. The stabilizers were merely overhauled and their hydraulics replaced.

An early decision had been to bring her up to

full MCA standard, to fit a larger, more powerful bowthruster aft of the bulbous bow and to add 3m (9ft 10in) to the stern in order to provide a modern bathing platform with twin curving stairways from the main deck. The stern extension also made room for a big lazarette wherein a new shore-power converter and a laundry room were installed along with storage for sports equipment. Space was found for a concealed hydraulic passerelle and underwater floodlights were inserted below the bathing platform.

**Above:** one of the spacious guest staterooms, finished in burr maple and adjoined to a Carrara marble bathroom

**Below:** the main saloon was recreated by London-based interior designer, Lindsay Jacobs

## SPECIFICATIONS

**LOA**
42.0m (137ft 10in)

**BEAM**
8.28m (27ft 2in)

**DRAUGHT**
2.5m (8ft 2in)

**DISPLACEMENT**
360 tons

**CONSTRUCTION**
Welded steel hull, aluminium alloy superstructure

**PROPULSION**
2 x Caterpillar 3412E, derated to 1,000hp

**GENERATORS**
2 x Kohler 65kVa

**FUEL**
54,000 litres

**WATER**
8,600 litres

**SPEED (MAX)**
16.5 knots

**RANGE @ 12 KNOTS**
3,000nm

**CLASSIFICATION**
ABS/Cayman Islands commercial registry, MCA compliant

**REFIT NAVAL ARCHITECT**
Cichero Aldo/Mondo Marine

**REFIT INTERIOR**
Lindsay Jacobs

**BUILDER/YEAR**
Mondo Marine/1991

**REFIT/YEAR**
Marsic Shipyard/2000-2001
Via L Cibrario
16154, Genova, Italy
Tel:+39 010 6506600
Fax:+39 010 6512651
Email: massimo@marsic.it

**PRINCIPAL EQUIPMENT**
Generators: Kohler
Stabilizers: Najad 300 series
Bowthruster: LHT 83kW
Air-conditioning: Frigit
Desalinators: Hydromar
Power converters: Atlas 50

The MCA requirements called for improved watertight bulkheads up to main deck level, additional emergency exits from the lower deck, fire-alarms and sprinklers as well as numerous other smaller changes and improvements.

All the guest accommodation was rebuilt, using the original burr maple panelling where possible. The aft section of the lower deck was restructured to provide two big VIP staterooms, one of which has a sitting area that can be partitioned off to make an additional small cabin if required. A pair of twin cabins forward of the engine room and the owner's suite on the main deck were rebuilt more or less as before, except that everything other than the basic structure and some of the joinery is new. All the cabins have en suite Carrara marble bathrooms, one of the special features of the yachts.

The crew accommodation, forward on the lower deck, was replanned and rebuilt to provide three twin en suite cabins and a crew mess. The captain, however, enjoys a cabin adjacent to the bridge.

The bridge itself was totally rebuilt using burr maple joinery and blue Connolly hide facings and overhead, while a completely new outfit of navigation and communications electronics was installed.

London-based interior designer Lindsay Jacobs recreated the saloon and dining room and selected the new carpets, marbles and soft furnishings for the whole yacht. A striking feature is a glass dividing screen between the two rooms etched with a design based on a Chagall painting in the possession of the owner. Forward of the dining room on the port side is a brand new all-electric galley, finished in brushed stainless steel with marble worktops.

Meanwhile the old teak decks were stripped off and rusty areas of the steel beneath were repaired to receive new teak on all decks except the sun deck. The old mast was removed and a new one carrying Satcom and television aerial domes was designed and installed further aft. This yacht has a notably large proportion of deck space compared to some newer designs, for in addition to the sun deck she has full walk-round decks at both main and boat deck levels. There are three very good alfresco dining areas on board and, with the tenders in the water, a very large space which is ideal for cocktail parties.

The entire yacht was primed, faired and painted in white Awlgrip gloss paint with a final topcoat being applied after all the other jobs were completed.

In June 2001, the vessel that had limped into Genoa as *Antares I* finally emerged as the pristine *Elenesse II*. A valid point that is often made about really major refits such as this one is that the final result is actually superior to a brand new yacht. That is because every problem that could possibly arise has already done so and been corrected. It is amazing to encounter such a relatively young vessel undergoing such an extensive refit, but there is little doubt that *Elenesse II* is now a much more impressive vessel than *Antares I* ever was, in every way.

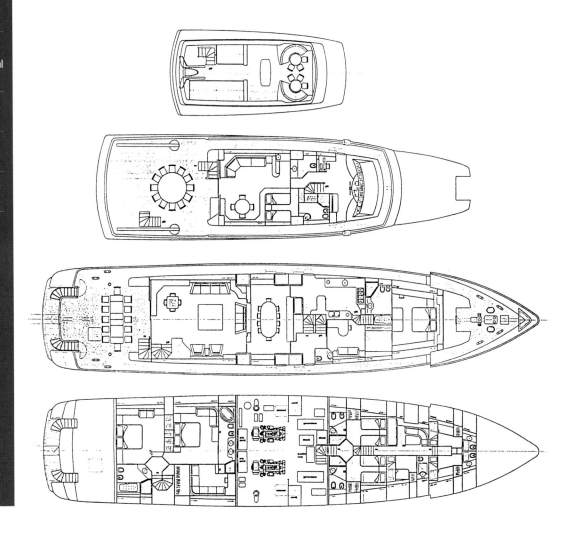

# Tamer II

**Below:** *Tamer II,* making good headway in Dutch waters shortly after her launch in 1986

The magnificent cruising yachts built in Holland by Jongert have a well-deserved reputation for quality. They are carefully designed and very well-built from the finest materials. Their interior fitting out and finish is at least as good if not better than any other series-produced yachts. But even a Jongert does not last for ever. The ceaseless attack by sea-water and hot sunshine will gradually break down even the best paint and will dry and crack the most superior teak decks. Constant use will wear out carpets, and sunshine will bleach the colours out of fabrics. Rubber gaskets will harden, varnish will be scuffed.

When the time comes for a refit, the owner will not want his yacht to go to just any yard and price may not be the only consideration. More likely he will choose one that has the builder's approval and has worked on other Jongerts before. Amico & Co of Genoa works as a service

point for Royal Huisman, Jongert and Wally yachts – three of the best-known sailing yacht lines on the market.

Built in 1986, the 36m (118ft) Jongert ketch *Tamer II* has cruised very extensively all over the world without actually doing a complete circumnavigation. Recently she spent three years in the Pacific and cruised both east and west coasts of the United States of America. The oceans of the world have been her home. Returning to the Mediterranean in 2000 she became due for a Lloyd's four-year survey and the owner decided that this was the right time to bring her back to 'as new' condition.

She arrived in Genoa during October 2000, with the usual request of having her ready for cruising next summer. Amico, which does not build new yachts but concentrates purely on refit and repair, works on roughly 120 yachts each year and *Tamer II* had to be fitted into an intricate schedule that included seven

other major refits and 10 full spray paint jobs.

After being lifted out of the water by Amico's 350 ton Travelift, *Tamer II* was placed initially on the outdoor hardstanding while all 'dirty' jobs were done. The most important of these was stripping back the old teak deck in order to replace it with a brand new one. As well as the teak, the existing plywood substrate was removed and the steel deck surface sand-blasted to bare metal. This is a very important stage because there are almost always some spots of rust that need correcting before the whole area is treated with primer.

Another task for the outdoors was pulling out the two masts and all of the rigging. These were taken into one of the sheds to be completely dismantled and overhauled, a job that could go on steadily through the winter. The spars themselves were due to be painted at the same time as the yacht, but first they were carefully

examined, small cracks were rewelded and spots of corrosion eliminated. After painting was completed, the yard riggers began the long job of replacing standing and running rigging, using new materials wherever needed.

One of the secrets of achieving a perfect paint job is to remove as many fittings as possible so that the steel or aluminium will be painted underneath them. In *Tamer II*'s case every single fitting that was possible to remove was taken off, including all the windows, which in due course would be replaced onto new gaskets. All skylights and deck hatches came off as well, the latter being substituted for new ones of an improved design which do not project so far. Those fittings that were painted were rubbed down and spray-painted in the yard's own paint cabin.

In order to reduce the possibility of blistering problems in the future, some of the interfaces between painted steel

**Above:** *Tamer II,* berthed outside Amico, displaying her smartly repainted topsides and sparkling white superstructure

**Right:** painting is carried out in a custom-built shed, which is equipped with heating, an overspray recovery plant with active carbon filters and special lighting

**Below:** both the propeller and propeller shaft were dismantled and overhauled

**Below right, centre and bottom:** seams between the teak planking were filled with rubber compound before being sanded off to result in a perfect finish

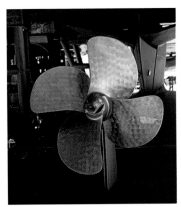

and teak deck and between the aluminium and wooden superstructure were taken back to bare metal and the design improved before priming and fairing.

A complete repaint was one of the two really major operations. Amico is an official Awlgrip application centre with all procedures following that company's recommendations. Painting takes place inside a custom-built shed which is equipped with heating, an overspray recovery plant with active carbon filters and special lighting. The work is constantly surveyed by the yard's quality control system and periodically by Awlgrip experts. *Tamer II* received a full topside respray in 'flag blue' while superstructures, masts and booms were painted white.

Before getting on to the final stage of painting, the replacement of the deck could proceed, with the yacht still under cover. The first task was to lay down a 15mm marine ply base which is fixed to the steel structure with stainless steel bolts and bedded on rubber compound. At this stage some improvements to the original decks could be made. In the central cockpit, for instance, the deck was given a slight camber to encourage water to drain away quickly while in other areas the surface was faired prior to applying the teak planks to ensure that the final appearance would be perfect. A special feature is that all the plywood areas are edged with solid teak to prevent any end-grain water penetration in future.

Next the teak itself, which was especially selected, straight-grained and colour matched in narrow 16mm-thick planks, was glued to the deck. Margin pieces were hand-made to fit around deck hardware and hatches. The new hatches were a big improvement because they project only slightly above the surface which makes walking on deck much more pleasant than before. Seams were filled with rubber compound and, after the correct curing period, the entire deck was sanded off to a perfect finish. In total, some 180m² (1,937sqft) of deck was renewed and this job alone involved more than three months work.

*Tamer II* was in good condition mechanically and only required some relatively minor improvements. The propeller shaft and propeller were dismantled and overhauled, and all bearings renewed. Likewise the rudder was taken down and all bearings regenerated or sleeved to correct dimensions while the steering gear hydraulic cylinders were serviced and packing replaced.

The main engine only required its regular servicing but the electronic remote control system was replaced with an improved model. A tricky problem on all cruising yachts is the storage of gasoline for use in outboard motors. It has to be stored so that any vapour

**Left:** the main saloon retains the same layout as before, but has been completely refurbished with new carpets, curtains and soft furnishings

**Below:** the magnificent owner's stateroom, which is a key feature of the Jongert design, looking pristine with new overhead panels and fabrics

from spilled fuel drains safely overboard and it has to be protected from excessive heat. *Tamer II*'s captain wanted to improve the existing storage so Amico engineers built a stainless steel tank to fit inside the starboard deck locker which has overboard drains. As a further safety enhancement the locker was then fitted with a vapour detection system which sets off a visual and sound alarm in the wheelhouse if any trace of gasoline leaks out.

Two existing shore-line handling capstans were replaced with new hydraulic ones. In the aft cockpit a larger refrigerator was fitted and this in turn called for a new teak cabinet to contain it. On deck the mainsheet track was removed and substitued for a fixed block system, and a stern davit was removed.

In the wheelhouse, specialist contractors installed a suite of new electronic systems including radar and navigational computers. Although the electronics were not Amico's responsibility, the yard joiners were called upon to tidy up the woodwork around new displays.

Down below, the furniture in two cabins was replaced completely, carefully maintaining the existing style and colouring of the yacht while other smaller joinery work was carried out throughout the yacht. It is inevitable that fabric overhead panels gradually become discoloured, especially when a yacht spends time in hot and humid parts of the world. For this reason all of *Tamer II*'s overhead panels were taken down and replaced with new Alcantara.

The main saloon and dining area were completely refurbished with new carpets, curtains, upholstery and

other soft furnishings. The rounded settee in the main saloon was reupholstered in Connolly leather. Soft furnishings including bed heads, bed coverings, curtains and carpets were replaced in all the cabins. Materials and colours were selected according to the owner's choice and then the yard's own interior decorator sourced the correct fabrics and had them made up as required for the different compartments and supervised their fitting. This alone is a major task on a yacht of this size.

And finally *Tamer II* was re-rigged and relaunched looking as good as new. You could say that this was a 'normal' refit of the kind that Amico does many times each year. The thing that makes this type of refit work so demanding is that a very large number of potentially tricky operations have to be completed according to a strict schedule. The owner wants his yacht to be perfect and yet is impatient to go cruising again. The yard has to control the whole process in a very disciplined manner to ensure that everything goes according to plan. That is why owners rely more and more on specialists such as Amico to refit their yacht on time, on budget and exactly to their requirements.

## SPECIFICATIONS

**LOA**
36.00m (118ft)

**BEAM**
7.70m (25ft)

**DRAUGHT**
3.60m (12ft)

**SAIL AREA**
Main: 159.7m² (1,718sqft)
Mizzen: 70.7m² (761sqft)
Genoa: 318.6m² (3,428sqft)
Yankee: 216.8m² (2,333sqft)
Staysail: 81.2m² (874sqft)

**CONSTRUCTION**
Welded steel hull, aluminium superstructure

**PROPULSION**
Mercedes TBD 234-V12
478kW/650pk at 2,000rpm

**GENERATORS**
38kW AGAM & 80kW AGAM

**FUEL CAPACITY**
22,460 litres

**FRESH WATER CAPACITY**
6,100 litres

**SPEED UNDER POWER**
12.5 knots

**RANGE UNDER POWER @ 12 KNOTS**
855nm

**BUILDER/YEAR**
Jongert BV/1986

**REFIT/YEAR**
Amico & Co/2001
Via dei Pescatori
16128 Genova, Italy
Tel:+39 010 2470067
Fax:+39 010 247055
E-mail: amico.yard@amico.it

# Amico & Co

The company was established in 1991 and is relatively unusual in that it is involved only with the refit and repair of large yachts. The Amico family has been concerned for many years with ship repair in the city of Genoa and realized that the new industry of yacht service was constantly increasing and needed unique facilities which have to be much cleaner and more specialized than a general shipyard. It therefore established the new organization on a 25,000m² (269,000sqft) site at the southern end of the city, close to the International Fairground. A 350-ton Travelift, one of the largest in the Mediterranean at the time, was installed and six large halls built for under-cover repair and painting. These were all new purpose-built installations which do not suffer from the usual shipyard problems of dust and dirt from years of steelwork. The yard became an official application centre for Awlgrip painting systems and has a solid reputation as a service point for Jongert, Wally, Benetti, Codecasa, Feadship and Royal Huisman yachts. A short distance away from the main yard, Amico has the use of a covered and heated dry dock up to 72m (236ft) in length where vessels too large to be lifted and moved into a building can be repaired and painted under controlled conditions. A recent example is a 70m (230ft) Benetti, which was entirely repainted in only eight months, to the client's utmost satisfaction.

The business has been very successful and has grown by as much as 30 per cent per annum. *Tamer II* was painted inside its new 'soft-cover' shed of 1,200m² (12,912sqft) floor area, where the air is both heated and filtered.

Rather surprisingly for a new organization, Amico tackles wooden hulls in addition to the more usual steel, aluminium or plastics. In fact one of the great strengths of Genoa as a repair centre is that it has been the nucleus of shipbuilding and repair for centuries and both the newest and oldest skills can be found there. The yard employs approximately 50 people directly but when partners and contractors are taken into account, around 150 people are normally at work. The number of yachts worked on each year currently averages about 100 but this total is constantly increasing.

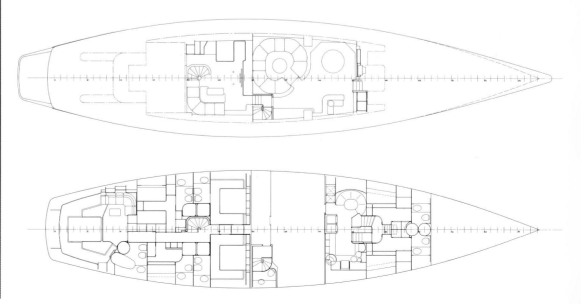

# RELAX

## "YOU'RE IN SAFE HANDS"

ENGINEERING • CARPENTRY • HAULOUTS • ANTI-FOULING • REFITS • UPHOLSTERY • ELECTRONICS • HYDRAULICS • RIGGING

Tel:(+34)971 718302 • Fax:(+34)971 718611
Palma de Mallorca • Spain

e.mail: info@boatyardpalma.com
www.boatyardpalma.com

**boat yard palma**

# Lady Vista

**Right:** formerly an ice-classed Swedish minelayer heavily constructed in steel, *Lady Vista* has now been converted into a luxury superyacht capable of cruising extensively in the most challenging conditions

**Below:** the Interboat 4.8m (16ft) launch with a 15hp inboard diesel engine

For the owner seeking to create a yacht with some kind of special purpose, conversion of a military vessel can provide a sensible, quick and cost-effective option. The navies of the world tend to build to the highest possible standards but when ships are no longer required they are sold for very reasonable prices.

A British businessman who has owned several motor yachts of the usual fast Mediterranean type decided to try something completely different. Instead of dashing from port to port, he yearned for a really seaworthy yacht that could take all conditions, cruise off the beaten track and remain self-sufficient for an extended period. This, in fact, is the concept of the 'Expedition yacht' which a number of builders have promoted, but conversion of an existing hull seemed to offer the prospect of obtaining more boat for the money.

The first step was to contact the specialist broker John Hughes and Associates with a request for a strong, characterful hull of around 30m (98ft) overall length suitable for conversion. Hughes quickly came up with a real gem – a 31m (102ft) ice-classed Swedish minelayer with diesel-electric propulsion. Built in the Swedish Navy's own dockyard in 1954, she was very solidly constructed in steel and was in first-class order throughout. Her task had been to lay mines in the Swedish archipelago to prevent Soviet submarines from infiltrating the Baltic, but with the end of the 'cold war' this became a remote possibility.

She was a pretty strange looking vessel, with a superstructure that was narrow at main deck level to make room for twin railway tracks for moving the mines around and big cranes at the bow and

stern for lifting them. However when all this was removed, a chunky but attractive hull remained. She is massively strong, heavily framed with ice reinforcement at the waterline and bows and with hull plating of 7 to 11mm. Below, there were two big holds for carrying the mines and a special system for rapidly flooding these in case of fire. Propulsion was twin screw driven by two large DC electric motors. These were powered by two Scania diesels, renewed in 1993 and there were two further auxiliary generators. In addition to being smooth and quiet, this system has the benefit of extreme flexibility of operation: the vessel can run on one screw or two, powered by one motor or two.

Thirty men formed her crew and a great deal of their time was spent on maintenance, resulting in a ship that was in very good condition considering her age. She was sold almost as soon as she came out of service in 1999 and was never laid up.

Having made the purchase, the new owner set about replanning the vessel. Acting as his own project manager in conjunction with his captain was part of the appeal, but recognizing the limitations

of this approach, various consultants including Design Anglia (Lowestoft) Ltd and Sir JH Biles (Naval Services) were employed. An early decision was to go for full Lloyd's approval and MCA certification. These certificates ensure that the conversion is completed to a recognized standard of seaworthiness but also make the yacht more saleable. However the cost and extra work involved are considerable.

Having completed a basic specification, the work was put out for tender and contracts signed with Forth Estuary Engineering, a small Scottish yard that is part of the Semple Cochrane Group. Shortly afterwards, the vessel was motored over from Sweden under her own power without any problems arising. As the idea of diesel-electric propulsion was unfamiliar, the owner had been considering removing the electric drives and turning the diesels around to drive the shafts directly. However, experts he consulted were unanimous in urging him to leave things as they were, as the diesel-electric system has many advantages and was working perfectly. Her top speed is 11 knots and she

**Left:** *Lady Vista* as she was as a working vessel. The entire superstructure, with the exception of the pilothouse, was replaced during refit

**Right:** large square windows allow plenty of natural light to filter into the modern-looking, fully-equipped galley

**Below:** the pilothouse was given a complete refurbishment and now boasts new mahogany woodwork and an extensive array of navigational equipment

cruises economically at 10, totally oblivious to all but the worst weather.

He had also been surprised to find that the main diesel engines and generators were bolted directly onto steel structural members without flexible mountings – normally a recipe for structure-born noise and vibration. However, during her trials in Sweden and her delivery to Britain, very low levels of vibration were noted, probably due to the ship's massive and stiff structure. It was felt that installing flexible mounts would bring little improvement, an opinion that was confirmed by acoustic specialists. Installation of soundproof sheeting throughout the engine room has been extremely effective in reducing airborne noise, resulting in a very quiet ship. Additional dampers were installed in the main engine air intakes and to the engine room extraction louvres, further reducing the noise transmitted to the deck.

An early task was to re-arrange the tankage. In her original configuration, when she had a large crew, equal amounts of fuel and fresh water (18,000 litres of each) were carried. By fitting two watermakers, the requirement for storing fresh water could be reduced to about 3,000 litres and the fuel capacity increased to 35,000 litres, giving a calculated range of 4,000 nautical miles at cruising revs. A further 2,000 litres of fresh water is stored in the forepeak and acts as a trim tank or for washing down while cruising.

In the engine room, one of the two auxiliary generators was removed and replaced by a new G&M generator in a hush-box which will ensure that *Lady Vista* will be very quiet when at anchor. Fortunately the engine room is quite large so there was no special difficulty in putting in the usual 'hotel' services: air-conditioning, central heating and vacuum-flush heads. Koopnautic stabilizers were installed as were a fuel centrifuge and an oily-water separator. Lloyd's required the main engines to be opened up for inspection: they were found to be perfect and reassembled without any work being needed.

The whole of the superstructure, including the bridge, was cut off at deck level and raised by 150mm to give more internal height, allowing the installation of insulated floating floors. By extending the new steel structure forward of the bridge, it was possible to increase the space available for the owner's accommodation and also to incorporate a Portuguese bridge. As a result there are full walk-round decks at both main and bridge levels. The owner quite rightly concluded that it would be out of character and inconvenient to have a full-width superstructure on this type of hull.

Aft of the bridge, a new upper saloon was constructed in aluminium. With large rectangular windows on either side and glazed double doors, this amply lives up to its nickname of 'the sun lounge'. Outside there is a good-sized teak deck with plenty of room for an extending teak table where alfresco meals can be taken under the shelter of an umbrella.

**Above:** double doors open out from the upper saloon on to a teak deck, which is the perfect spot for alfresco dining

**Below:** the minelayer had railways along each side, leading to launching points at the stern

**Bottom:** cranes at the bow and stern were used for lifting the mines

**Above:** the dining room adopts a simple and elegant style

**Below:** the tongue-and-groove styled ceilings and traditional ports create a nautical feel in the owner's stateroom

The roof of the upper saloon provides further deck space for sunbathing.

The two tenders are carried on the foredeck and launched by a hydraulic crane. One is a RIB, which is fast enough for water-skiing, but as the owner's wife had said she was tired of arriving ashore in wet clothes, the other is a pretty little Dutch launch with inboard diesel and folding pram-hood to provide more civilized transport.

The accommodation has been fitted out in a simple, unfussy modern style that seems very appropriate for the type of vessel. The steel decks are cambered and although the amount of camber was reduced somewhat in installing plywood floating floors, it is still noticeable and adds character to the interior. Maintaining this theme, tongue-and-groove styled ceilings have been used with false beams at intervals. On the main deck, mahogany joinery is complemented by white carpets and upholstery.

A doorway on the port side of the main saloon leads forward to a very attractive modern galley with all electric equipment and a splendid view of the seascape through the large windows. The owner's stateroom occupies the traditional position forward on the main deck and has two very smart bathrooms with individual shower cubicles. Rather surprisingly, Lloyd's insisted on traditional ports with storm-covers for the forward bulkhead and the owner was at pains to point out that this was a requirement rather than a slightly exaggerated styling feature.

In a reversal of the usual arrangement, the four guest cabins are forward on the lower deck. Two are conventional en suite double cabins and the other two are en suite twins with an unusual but practical staggered layout of bunks to suit the taper of the bow.

The three crew have cabins aft of the engine room as well as a surprisingly large crew mess and basic galley. A special feature of the layout is that it is possible to reach any part of the accommodation without going on deck, which might be a useful safety feature in bad weather.

The upper saloon is a bright, sunny compartment which is furnished with light-toned limed oak woodwork, a white carpet and blue-grey leather settees. With its splendid views in three directions and a full audio-visual outfit, it is bound to be a favourite place to relax.

Forward, past a day head, one reaches the bridge which has a very professional feel with its forward-sloping trawler-style windows. Although the original structure was retained, everything else is new, including the mahogany woodwork and a complete outfit of controls and navigational equipment. On the port side there is a navigation and communications centre where all the

additional equipment required by MCA such as fire alarms, water-tight door closure and GMDSS is installed.

The owner paid particular tribute to the electrical installation by Semple Cochrane, which is of the highest professional standard.

When the owner is aboard he acts as captain, however the yacht is designed for charter, in which case an additional, fourth crew member would be taken on. It is the present owner's intention to enjoy the vessel for a while and then put her on the market. With her ruggedly good-looking appearance, super-strong hull and the endorsement of both Lloyd's and MCA, she should represent an excellent investment.

## SPECIFICATIONS

**LOA**
31.20m (102ft 4in)

**BEAM**
7.40m (24ft 3in)

**DRAUGHT**
2.40m (7ft 10in)

**DISPLACEMENT**
230 tonnes

**CONSTRUCTION**
Ice reinforced steel hull and main deck superstructure, aluminium bridge and upper saloon

**PROPULSION**
2 x Scania DS11 rated at 188kW @ 1,800rpm linked to ASEA 142kW DC electric

**GENERATORS**
1 Scania 120kVA, 1 G&M 72kVA

**SPEED (MAX)**
11 knots

**RANGE @ 10 KNOTS**
Approx 4,000nm

**CLASSIFICATION**
Lloyd's ⊕100A1 Yacht, LMC, MCA

**NAVAL ARCHITECT**
Swedish Navy

**BUILDER/YEAR**
Marinerkstaderna, Stockholm /1954

**REFIT NAVAL ARCHITECT**
Construction: Design Anglia (Lowestoft) Ltd
Stability: Sir JH Biles (Naval Services) Ltd

**REFIT INTERIOR DESIGN**
Owner/captain

**REFIT YARD**
Forth Estuary Engineering Ltd/2001
Edinburgh Dock, Leith
Edinburgh, Scotland, UK
Tel:+44 (0)131 554 6434
Fax:+44 (0)131 555 1890

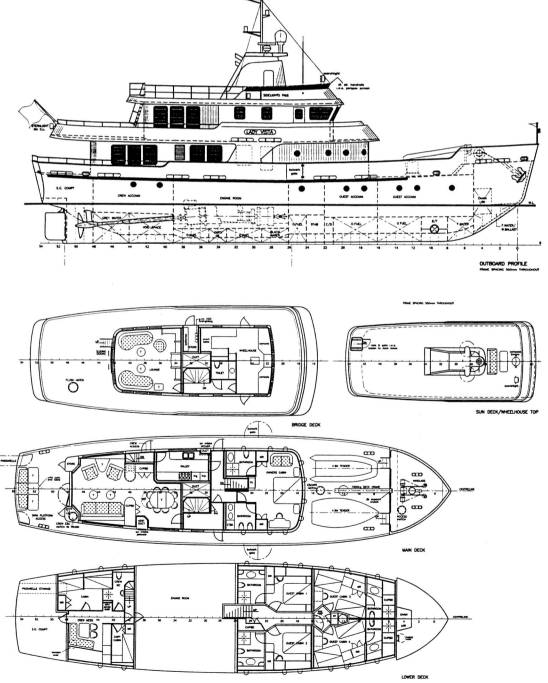

# Shamrock V

**Right:** *Shamrock V* is undoubtedly one of the most beautiful yachts to grace the seas. Since her refit at Pendennis Shipyard, her boat speed is much improved, she accelerates more quickly and is more sensitive on the helm

**Below right:** *Shamrock V* and her crew taking part in Antigua Classic Week in 1999

A few years ago it was possible to take a sightseeing trip on the River Hamble, the most yacht-crowded of the rivers that flow into The Solent off the South Coast of England. To attract customers the boatman would shout 'see the famous J-Class yachts *Endeavour* and *Velsheda*', though in truth the two old hulks stuck in their mud-berths were a somewhat pitiful sight. At that time, everyone imagined that the 'J' Class was extinct – fabulous monsters from a vanished golden age of yachting.

However they were wrong, as first *Endeavour* and later *Velsheda* were dragged from the mud and completely rebuilt to begin a second life as racing and cruising yachts *par excellence*. What many people forgot was that, of the 10 'J' Class built, one more, namely *Shamrock V*, still survived and now she has also been fully restored there are three genuine 'J' Class, all in first-class order. What makes *Shamrock V* so very special is the fact that she was the very first 'J' Class to be built. Sir Thomas Lipton made five challenges for the America's Cup, the last being in 1930. After protracted negotiations it had been agreed that instead of using handicaps as before, the America's Cup races should in future be 'boat for boat' using 'J' Class of the Universal Rule; a formula involving waterline length, sail area and displacement. A very important point was that the yachts had to meet Lloyd's scantling rules which

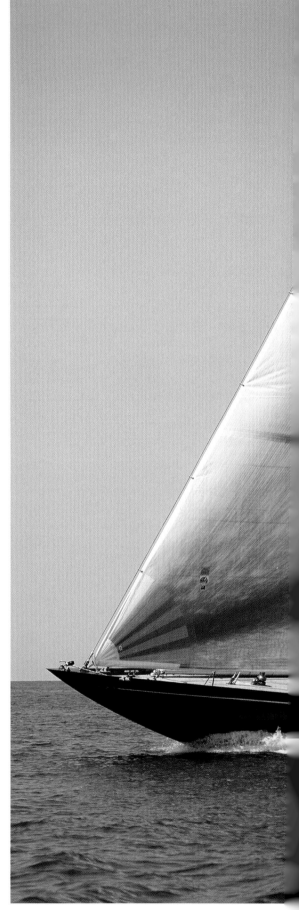

**Right:** ultra-sounding of her steelwork revealed that some of the strapping and framework were wasted and therefore needed replacing

**Below right:** Fairlie Restorations constructed the deckhouse to closely resemble the original

**Bottom right:** a new stainless steel rudder is partly filled with oil to give it neutral buoyancy, resulting in a light helm

see the Second World War on the horizon, pulled off a smart deal by selling *Shamrock V* to the Italian newspaper publisher Mario Crespi who renamed her *Quadrifoglio* and converted her to ketch rig. Because he was a friend of Mussolini, Crespi managed to lay the yacht up safely ashore for the duration of the war and she thus avoided the fate of most racing yachts; being broken up for the lead in their keels.

Even so, she only just escaped that fate after Crespi's death when Piero Scanu came upon her by chance in Genoa when she was in a very poor state. On being told that she was due to be broken up a few days later Scanu

meant that the defender could not gain an advantage by building an ultra-light hull that would not have survived a passage across the Atlantic. It also ensured that *Shamrock V* was well built, helping to guarantee her survival to the present day.

*Shamrock V* was designed by Charles E Nicholson and built by Camper & Nicholsons at Gosport of mahogany planking on steel frames with a hollow spruce mast. Unfortunately her opponent in the cup races proved to be a much more advanced design, the most innovative of that period. *Enterprise*, designed by Starling Burgess, was one of the very first yachts to have a hollow aluminium alloy mast, calculated to be over 2,000lbs lighter than *Shamrock V*'s, and she also introduced the 'Park Avenue boom' which enabled the mainsail shape to be controlled by a series of transverse tracks with adjustable stops on them. *Enterprise*, sailed by Mike Vanderbilt, retained the America's Cup by four races to nil.

After returning to England, *Shamrock V* had several owners in quick succession. TOM Sopwith bought her as a test-bed in preparation for his own 1934 challenge with *Endeavour*, and when that yacht began building sold her again to Richard Fairey, who at first sailed her as tuning partner for *Endeavour* and then sent her back to Camper & Nicholsons for conversion to a cruiser/racer. This provided three cabins aft, crew quarters forward and an elegant saloon fitted out in bird's-eye maple.

In 1937 Fairey, who as an aircraft-manufacturer could

made an immediate offer to buy her. Not only did Scanu save her from destruction, he restored her cutter rig and used her as a family cruising yacht for 17 years. At the end of this time he sent her back to Camper & Nicholsons who carried out a major rebuild in 1978, the last to be completed at their Southampton Shipyard, now renamed Shamrock Quay.

During that refit her very tired mahogany planking was replaced with teak and she was given new engines, deckhouse, bulwarks and a new rig, while the interior built for Richard Fairey was carefully restored. After this refit, Scanu kept *Quadrifoglio* for a further 10 years before selling her to the Lipton Tea Company, who in 1985 gave her to the Newport Museum of Yachting. In due course she passed back into private ownership via the International Yacht Restoration School and now has an owner whose ambition is to race on level terms with the other two 'J's – as well as any new ones that might come along in the future. To make this possible *Shamrock V* needed a further major refit with three principal aims; firstly to ensure that she became a sound and seaworthy racing and cruising yacht, capable of crossing the oceans in safety and meeting modern cruising needs. Secondly she was to be restored as closely as possible to her original appearance while conceding that modern deck equipment and fittings would be used, and finally that her performance should be broadly similar to the other two 'J' Class, so that racing between them would be competitive.

The yard selected for this very exacting task was Pendennis Shipyard at Falmouth where the work was carried out initially under the supervision of Elizabeth Meyer and later her captain Thom Perry, while Gerry Dijkstra, who has been involved with all three of the yachts, acted as consultant naval architect working under the classification rules of ABS.

The most major structural repair was the replacement of a steel keel box which had been installed in 1978 and was suffering from corrosion. You cannot flip a yacht this size upside down, so to replace the keel she was suspended

from her own beam shelf which was welded to a pair of massive 8-inch 'I' beams that transferred the load to a support structure. She actually remained 'airborne' in this way for a whole year while work proceeded.

A completely new steel box structure was built, incorporating various water and fuel tanks, and below this a new hollow steel keel into which the original lead ballast was poured. Meanwhile the whole of the interior accommodation had been removed to give access to the hull structure. The 1978 teak planking was still perfect but some of the steel framing needed to be repaired or replaced, especially the bilge stringer and some of the sole margin plates. In spite of this, approximately 60 per cent of her steel structure remains original, making her by far the most authentic of the three yachts.

In one of his experiments to improve *Shamrock V*'s performance, Richard Fairey had arranged to have the original stern post cut through and a new one fitted

**Above:** *Shamrock V*'s 1934 accommodation had to be totally replaced with a brand new interior

**Below:** her topsides were splined, faired and then painted in the traditional green that had identified all of Sir Thomas Lipton's challengers

began by carefully fairing the steel structure with appropriate packing pieces before applying a 30mm plywood deck which formed the base for 18mm of teak.

Although *Velsheda* was fitted with a carbon-fibre mast, this was felt to have been a mistake as it places additional stress on the structure, and *Shamrock V* has a more conventional, though still extremely impressive Rondal mast built from Alustar aluminium alloy. The triangular 'Park Avenue' boom on the other hand was built of carbon-fibre by Carbospars, as in this case its lightness reduces stress and makes handling it safer.

One of the major compromises with a refit of this kind is based on the fact that *Shamrock V* must be capable of sailing safely with just her nine permanent crew compared to 25 or so in her racing days. For this reason, powered winches are essential and some 20 are fitted on deck, four of which can be driven by a pair of 'coffee-grinder' pedestals and the remainder by hydraulic power. The modern 'J' Class permits the yachts to race with generators running to make this possible. An important innovation in

**Above and right:** the saloon and dining area retain the character of the original interior, with bird's-eye maple panelling and floors made from African afrormosia

**Far right:** the spacious master cabin in the stern comprises a desk and sofa to starboard and a double bed to port

**Below:** a winch coated with titanium nitride provides a bronze-like appearance and needs very little polishing

that shortened the chord of the rudder. Unfortunately the original timber was still in place but rotten after 70 years and therefore had to be cut out and replaced. For various reasons it proved impossible to retain the original wooden rudder and this was substituted for one made of stainless steel.

The 1978 planking had been sheathed in 'Cascover', a resin-bonded nylon product and this had started to come away in places. It was therefore stripped off, which also enabled the yard to see and check every single bronze fastening. In place of the Cascover, a new sheathing of e-glass was applied below the waterline while the topsides were splined, faired and painted in the traditional manner.

The deck was removed completely so that all the steelwork under it could be checked and repaired where necessary. Additional steel carlins and pillars were welded in to strengthen and stiffen the structure. Fairlie Restorations was given the task of replacing the deck and

*Shamrock V*'s case is that all the deck hardware, much of it specially built by Ian Terry, has been coated with titanium nitride to give it a bronze appearance instead of glittering stainless steel.

All mechanical and electrical systems are completely new as there was no point in retaining equipment of various vintages – none of it original. Instead of a single large motor driving a central propeller in a rudder cut-out, *Shamrock V* is powered by a pair of 205hp Caterpillars which drive MaxProp feathering propellers on either side of the rudder. The captain Thom Perry finds that these give all the manoeuvrability he needs and amply justifies the decision not to fit a bowthruster.

Of course a modern yacht requires a full range of 'hotel' equipment such as air-conditioning, unlimited fresh water, generous electricity supply and so on, and the Pendennis engineers found their ingenuity stretched to the limit to fit all the systems within a very limited space and still retain sufficient access for maintenance.

Not enough remained of the 1930s interior to restore and in any case the joinery had been found to contain woodworm in 1978 so a completely new interior has been fitted which is faithful to the spirit of the original. The saloon is once again panelled in bird's-eye maple with an afrormosia floor while the cabins have fiddleback mahogany panels and solid mahogany details. The guest accommodation has been rearranged to increase the number of cabins to four, including a spacious master cabin in the counter with a double bed, settee and elegant marble-trimmed en suite bathroom. A smaller double cabin and two twins brings the total number in the owner's party to eight. Of the crew only the captain enjoys a tiny private cabin; the other eight crew share the open-plan forecastle forward of the mast. To serve aboard this yacht therefore calls for considerable dedication in addition to exceptional levels of skill.

In commissioning this outstandingly thorough and, naturally, extremely expensive refit, the owner of *Shamrock V* had one very special aim in view; to race on level terms against *Endeavour* and *Velsheda*. For all the astronomical costs involved with such a project, to own and race a genuine 'J' Class must surely make you part of the most exclusive and rewarding club in the world.

## SPECIFICATIONS

LOA
36.42m (119ft 6in)

BEAM
6.00m (19ft 8in)

DRAUGHT
4.87m (16ft 0in)

BALLAST
60 tonnes

DISPLACEMENT
165 tonnes

SAIL AREA
1,600m2 (17,216sqft)

CONSTRUCTION
Composite: teak on steel
frames

PROPULSION
2 x Caterpillar 3116, 205hp

GENERATORS
2 x Northern Lights 25kW

FUEL CAPACITY
4,000 litres

CLASSIFICATION
ABS

NAVAL ARCHITECT
Charles E Nicholson

REFIT NAVAL ARCHITECT
Gerard Dijkstra

PROJECT MANAGEMENT
Thomas L Perry

BUILDER/YEAR
Camper & Nicholsons/1930

REFIT/YEAR
Pendennis Shipyard/2001
The Docks, Falmouth
Cornwall TR11 4NB, UK
Tel:+44 (0)1326 211344
Fax:+44 (0)1326 319253
Email: info@pendennis.com

PRINCIPAL EQUIPMENT
Spars: Rondal; Rigging: Navtec
Sails: Doyle; Gearbox: Twin Disc
Propellers: MaxProp
Hydraulic power-pack &
winches: Lewmar
Windlass: Maxwell
Watermakers: Village Marine

# PENDENNIS SHIPYARD

Lying beneath the ancient guns of Pendennis Castle in Falmouth, South-west England, Pendennis Shipyard is ideally situated on one of the country's largest and safest natural harbours. The yard was founded in 1989 by British entrepreneur Peter de Savary, who also commissioned its first major project, the 37.3m (122ft 8in) Dubois-designed sloop, *Taramber*, which was completed in 1991. Following a management buyout in 1994, Pendennis Shipyard has blended high quality new construction with comprehensive refits and rebuilds, while continuously improving its facilities and increasing its skilled workforce. Today, the yard can offer three climate-controlled construction halls, two of 70m (229ft) in length and one of 40m (131ft), a 70m (229ft) covered

dock for sail-in refit and repair, a 500 tonne slipway and a heavy duty travel lift. Its list of new builds includes the 42.6m (140ft) German Frers-designed, aluminium-hulled sloop *Rebecca*, the 47.7m (156ft) aluminium motor yacht *Ilona* and the 35m (115ft) aluminium ketch *Beagle V*, both of the latter designed by Ed Dubois. At the same time, highly prestigious refits and extensive rebuilds have been carried out on famous-name vessels such as the 56m (183ft) three-masted schooner *Adix*, the 46m (150ft) schooner *Adela*, and most recently the historic J-Class sloop *Shamrock V*.

Under the leadership of Managing Director Henk Wiekens, and Commercial Director Mike Carr, the yard employs a workforce of around 194 people.

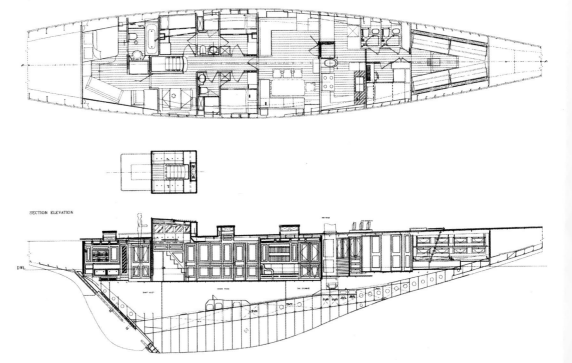

# Mayan Queen III

**Main picture:** *Mayan Queen III* looking brand new after her extensive refit. The owner and captain went to great lengths to establish exactly what alterations were needed before taking her to Derecktor of Florida

Many refit projects seem to escalate as they go along, starting with just a few simple changes and evolving into a time and money intensive operation which can strain both tempers and pocketbooks. Perhaps the most dangerous words in any refit are, 'as long as we're doing this, we might as well...' The refit of *Mayan Queen III*, however, is the exact opposite of an ill-defined project. With a business-like owner, a knowledgeable captain and a talented boatyard, the *Mayan Queen III* rebuild was done on budget and on time. Most significantly of all, everyone – the owner, captain and yard – were delighted with the finished yacht.

The starting point for *Mayan Queen III* was as the

Feadship build number 764, launched in 1990 as *Alfa Alfa III*. She was later renamed *Kisses*. A 45.5m (149ft) motor yacht designed by Frits de Voogt and built by Van Lent & Zonen, she reflected the decor of the 1980s and early 1990s with a glitzy interior of glass, chrome and gold. The owner of *Mayan Queen II*, a 40m (132ft) Hakvoort, was looking for a larger yacht and discovered that *Kisses* was for sale. However rather than just buying the yacht and then deciding how to make her fit his needs, the methodical owner took a wiser and more disciplined course. First, with his family and Captain Scott Marina, he took his Hakvoort, *Mayan Queen II*, to the Atlantis resort and berthed next to the then-*Kisses*. The prospective owner liked the

stern to move a passerelle that forced a low ceiling in one of the guest staterooms and to create a larger swimming platform but, as a result of the time spent aboard, a number of other changes were also desired.

Three separate refits were conceived, and the owner considered each one, looking at sketches and drawings as well as estimates of cost and the amount of time needed. Once a decision was made on what would be done, bids were solicited from a number of boatyards. Dutch yards were seriously considered but the owner, with a boating history that included a Trumpy, Burger and the Hakvoort, wanted to be involved in the refit and decided that it was too far to travel frequently to European yards. The choice of Derecktor Gunnell in Fort Lauderdale, Florida was made not only on the basis of the craftsmanship needed or the cost involved, but also on the personal relationship that the owner and captain had already built up with the management team during a refit of the Hakvoort.

Unforeseeably Derecktor Gunnell went through a change in ownership shortly after *Mayan Queen III* started the refit in late 1999, with some of the owner's friends leaving the yard. Nevertheless, the work at the renamed Derecktor of Florida never faltered and the 15-month project ended seamlessly, without any problems.

Certainly the key to the success of the *Mayan Queen III* refit was the comprehensive planning done beforehand. As Captain Marina points out, 'almost nothing was changed from the original plan that Derecktor Gunnell bid on, so there were

**Below:** as *Alfa Alfa III*, *Mayan Queen III* was originally built in 1990 by Van Lent & Zonen, Holland, with an interior designed by Robert Knack

basic concept of this Feadship and consequently he and his captain went back and forth, discussing and even measuring up potential changes. During this whole process, they were also making contact with the F de Voogt design office to establish the possibilites of their proposals and the costs likely to be involved. This led to a five day charter of *Kisses* in the Bahamas, where more ideas and changes were noted and an overall plan was conceived. The yacht was purchased in May 1999 and once again she cruised the Caribbean while the new owner and his skipper decided how to proceed with the refit.

With a host of ideas, they ended up at de Voogt Yacht Service, which specializes in rebuilds of Feadships. The basic goal was to modify the

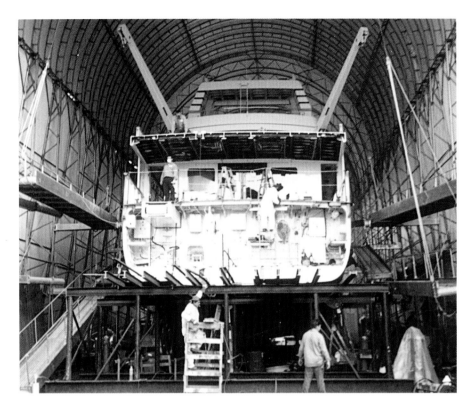

The new aft section was built by Derecktor on site, framed out from the truncated hull and flawlessly fitted and finished. The stretched section also created an enormous air-conditioned lazarette, which was put to good use. It holds an extra washer and dryer and, since it opens directly to the transom platform, has a spacious storage area set aside for scuba gear. The dive tanks can be filled while in racks and there is a storage locker for wetsuits as well. A refrigerator and icemaker provide supplies for the tender, while a davit assembles to disembark the twin motor-bikes. From tender docklines to rods and reels, everything has a place and is neatly secured.

Unlike many hull stretches, de Voogt and the owner decided to move the running gear as well. The propeller shafts were extended roughly 1.5m (4.9ft) aft, and Van Lent fabricated new steering and larger rudders. The keel was lengthened, the former propeller pockets were filled in, and a third strut was added to support the shaft. The result under way is, according to Captain Marina, a vastly transformed yacht which both tracks and turns better than before. The stretched after section required the boat deck to be extended, which was also fabricated by Derecktor,

**Above and right:** the largest aspect of *Mayan Queen III*'s refit was the complete replacement of the stern, increasing her overall length by 3.08m (10ft)

no surprises for either the owner or the yard.'

The most obvious and the largest part of the refit was the removal of the entire transom, which was then thrown away and replaced by a completely new stern. In the process, the yacht was stretched from 45.5m (149ft) to 48.58m (160ft). The new stern is innovative, with a curving staircase on the starboard side and an extended walkway to the repositioned passerelle to port. The 'wings' on each side extend the lines of the hull and provide a well-protected area for boarding the tenders as well as a spacious swimming platform.

while Teak Decking Systems matched up the teak to create an enormous deck which would easily be able to carry a pair of tenders, including a 7.3m (24ft) Intrepid, a Novurania and a pair of personal watercraft. Derecktor also extended the polished steel rail around the boat deck, matching it perfectly.

One method that the owner and captain used to ensure that everything turned out properly was to test all the layout changes beforehand, using thin veneers to make inexpensive mock-ups of the planned additions. This allowed them to check for clearances, heights and general appearance before the craftsmen started their work.

One of the most visible layout changes was the expansion of the sky lounge. The entire aft bulkhead, including the doors and windows, was created by Freeman Marine in Seattle using measurements taken at Derecktor and, when shipped to the yacht, it was welded perfectly in place. Lighthouse Shipwrights finished the new sky lounge with an entertainment centre and new carpentry. The original yacht unusually had no day head serving the sky lounge, so this was one aspect which the owner certainly wanted changed. A head was fitted by stealing some space from the navigation area of the pilothouse, as well as from the captain's cabin.

The saloon was toned down to create a more comfortable look, with a new bar with granite counter top added aft to starboard. Craftsmen at Derecktor built all the new joinery for the saloon, dining areas and owner's suite, which matched the existing woodwork perfectly. The final appearance has achieved a more relaxing rather than glitzy environment. The aft deck, which leads on from the main saloon, received a big curved sofa facing twin tables on hydraulic lifts for dining or entertaining.

The owner's suite undoubtedly benefited from the refit done by Derecktor, with his-and-hers walk-in wardrobes added, a new office area created to starboard and the entire suite enlarged by pushing the panelling and carpentry outboard. The bathroom was completely renovated to replicate

**Left and below:** renovations to the aft deck included the installation of a curved sofa facing two hydraulically-lifting tables which can be used for dining alfresco. The large wicker chairs make it a comfortable area in which to relax

**Below right:** the main saloon used to feature large cushioned sofas upholstered in rich fabrics, with the ceiling comprising a combination of gold inlay, mirrors, lacquered wood and suede panelling

**Bottom:** during the refit a more muted colour scheme was chosen for the main saloon, creating a very relaxing environment

the older *Mayan Queen II*, with only the centre line bathtub remaining. New blue bahia granite was added, pewter fixtures were chosen rather than gold, and the ceilings were totally replaced. The stateroom also received a new entertainment system from Intelect Integrated Electronics.

Other modifications included new navigation and communication gear in the pilothouse by Island Marine Electronics, the addition of wet bars both on the boat deck and sun deck, and new stainless steel counters in the galley. While the yard work was under way, the engineer and crew stripped the engine room and bilge back to steel and painted the entire compartment with white Awlgrip. Unlike most refits, literally every item in

the engine room was removed, overhauled, painted and then reinstalled.

Captain Marina had carefully researched potential subcontractors so that, when the yacht arrived at Derecktor, he was ready to start a multitude of projects. Intelect Integrated Electronics computerized the stereo and entertainment systems throughout, Classic Yacht Refinishing faired and repainted the entire hull and Dart Canvas provided new exterior and interior upholstery. Powless Drapery Services carried out the work on the interior overheads, the wall panels in the guest staterooms, owner's suite, main saloon and sky lounge, as well as upholstered the bed bases and headboards, while Clint Yacht Refinishing restored all the interior wood. Nautilus

**Above:** alterations made to the owner's stateroom incorporated two new walk-in wardrobes and the installation of a new entertainment system. The dimensions of the entire suite were enlarged by moving the panelling and joinery outboard

**Left:** the owner's stateroom as it looked before being refurbished

provided the scuba compressor and systems, Beard Marine upgraded the air-conditioning with a 45-ton Marine Air system, Quantum Marine overhauled the stabilizers and installed a new Koopnautic system, underwater flood lights at the stern were added by Underwater Lights (USA) and Savage Lighting provided fibre-optic nameboards.

Not only did everyone have a thorough grasp of exactly what was wanted from the outset, but the captain was also fully prepared so that the clean-up afterwards was minimized. As a starting point, while the Derecktor yard was cutting off the stern, Captain Marina and his crew were stripping all the exterior varnish back to bare wood and then building up 10 coats of new varnish. Once finished, all the wood was carefully covered for protection from the elements and from stray nicks

caused by the work going on. Just before *Mayan Queen III* left Derecktor, the crew added one final coat of varnish, resulting in superbly finished exterior woodwork. Gibb Systems also routed and recaulked all the teak decking at the start of the project, but Captain Marina advised them to leave the extra rubber caulking on top of the teak to create a protective coating during the construction. Just before completion, the decks were sanded to finish off the caulking, culminating in immaculate decking as well.

Completed on budget and within days of the predicted finish date, *Mayan Queen III* is a perfect example of a refit which was accomplished with careful planning, an adherence to the overall programme, and a talented team of owner, captain and shipyard.

**Right:** the sky lounge is one of the most visible transformations on board, having been significantly expanded before receiving brand new carpentry and a day head

## SPECIFICATIONS

**LOA**
48.58m (159ft 4in)

**BEAM**
8.18m (26ft 10in)

**DRAUGHT**
2.64m (8ft 8in)

**DISPLACEMENT**
402 tonnes

**PROPULSION**
2 x Detroit Diesel 16V92TA

**SPEED**
14 knots

**GENERATORS**
2 x Detroit Diesel 95kW

**CONSTRUCTION**
Steel and aluminium

**CLASSIFICATION**
Lloyd's ✠100 A1

**NAVAL ARCHITECTURE**
de Voogt Yacht Service

**BUILDER/YEAR**
Van Lent & Zonen/1990

**REFIT/YEAR**
Derecktor of Florida/2000

775 Taylor Lane

Dania

Florida FL 33004

USA

Tel:+1 954 920 5756

Fax:+1 954 925 1146

E-mail:

sales@derecktor–florida.com

# Derecktor of Florida

Founded in 1967, Derecktor of Florida covers more than 17 acres on the Dania Cut Off Canal, which is conveniently located in close proximity to Fort Lauderdale's airport. Derecktor is a full service yard capable of accomplishing any project, from new builds and major refits through to the construction of carbon-fibre masts. Employing approximately 140 people, the yard's facilities include a 600 ton elevated platform with a rail transfer system and two travelifts at 160 tons and 60 tons respectively. There is also a 3,000 ton floating dry dock under construction. With the capacity to handle yachts up to 53.3m (175ft), Derecktor of Florida's aims are simple – to deliver quality work and exceed customer's expectations. These objectives therefore ensure advanced design, a high standard of craftsmanship and timely deliveries, all of which contribute to making Derecktor one of the finest full-service yards in Florida.

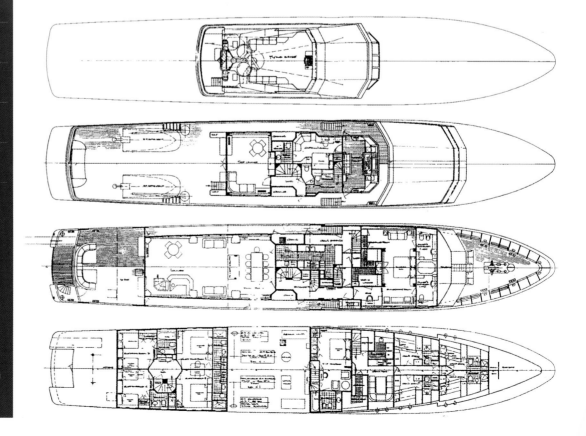

# DESTINATION: THE BEARD MARINE GROUP

*F*or more than 18 years, Beard Marine has sold and serviced the finest marine air conditioning, refrigeration and watermaker systems available. Our reputation for quality service and installations is paramount in the industry. No matter how big or how small the project, you can depend on the Beard Marine Group.

Don't let problems with your air conditioning, refrigeration and watermaker systems spoil your fun. The Beard Marine Group, headquartered in Fort Lauderdale with affiliated offices in Palm Beach and Savannah, is able to provide customers with the highest level of dependability while cruising along the Southeast Coast and the Caribbean.

**SPECIALIZING IN LARGE MEGA-YACHT RETRO-FIT PROJECTS**

**SERVICE ANYTIME. SERVICE ANYWHERE.**

The Beard Marine Group's courteous and professional staff and their commitment to excellence, assisted our refit to be completed in a manner which I command.
-- Captain Scott Marina
M/Y Mayan Queen

## THE BEARD MARINE GROUP
A/C • WATERMAKERS • REFRIGERATION

**800-663-7561**
Ft. Lauderdale: 954-463-2288 • Fax 954-527-0362
Palm Beach: 561-881-9598 • FAX 561-881-9599
Savannah: 912-356-5222 • FAX 912-692-1006

Visit our web site at: www.beardmarine.com

Sea Recovery®
*"The Watermakers That Work."*

MARINE AIR SYSTEMS®

# Wherever unfailing reliability is valued above all else.

*Take a lifetime of experience onboard.* It took us a lifetime to build our reputation as *the* marine electrical specialists. And as our team of world-class ABYC certified electricians continue to set new standards of technical proficiency, our reputation continues to spread. So that today yacht owners in ports of call around the globe can depend on our people and our equipment to be there as fast as humanly possible. Because for us it's not just a matter of pride. It's a matter of family tradition. A family tradition of unfailing reliability.

**WARD'S**
**MARINE ELECTRIC**
ESTABLISHED 1950

630 SW Flagler Ave. ■ Fort Lauderdale, Florida 33301-2837 ■ Phone: 954.523.2815 ■ Toll Free: 800.545.9273
Fax: 954.523.1967 ■ Toll Free Fax: 800.297.8240 ■ www.wardsmarine.com ■ e-mail: info@wardsmarine.com

# Alpha Marine Ltd.

NAVAL ARCHITECTS, MARINE CONSULTANTS AND SURVEYORS

Summit Furniture (Europe) Ltd.
198 Ebury Street, Orange Sq., London SW1W 8UN
*Telephone:* +44 (0)20 7259 9244    *Facsimile:* +44 (0)20 7259 9246

Summit Furniture, Inc.
5 Harris Court, Monterey, CA 93940
*Telephone:* 831.375.7811    *Facsimile:* 831.375.0940

# REFITS

## A LUXURY LOCATION WITH COST EFFECTIVE EXPERTISE

CAIRNS
AUSTRALIA

Cairns Slipways has been servicing luxury vessels since the early 1980's.
Now vessels travel the world to experience Cairns Slipways'
world class refit, repairs, paint refinishing and superior standard of shipwrights.

Cairns Slipways - a division of NQEA Australia Pty. Ltd.
18-22 Tingira Street, Portsmith, Cairns 4870 Australia  Intl. Tel: 61 7 4052 7354  Intl. Fax: 61 7 4035 2332
Email: cairns-slipways@nqea.com.au  Website: www.cairns-slipways.com.au

# The modular configuration, and infrared remote control, for example!

Modular design is an unique feature of the CLIMMA range of CWS central station chilled water air-conditioning systems. This division into individual refrigeration cells means that the chiller is far simpler to install and subsequently service.

*Illustrated:* **CLIMMA CWS 722 S RC** Chiller Maximum capacity 90,000 Bth/h. Two compressor of 3 HP each. The CWS air-conditioners range from 12,000 to 380,000 btus/h and include a complete range of ducted fan coils and boxed air handlers with individual temperature controls.

The VEGA infrared remote control is an unique feature of the CLIMMA range of CWS central station chilled water and Cabin stand-alone air-conditioners. The remote panel display shows all the important functions but still is very simple to operate and keeps in its memory all of the setting even after power failute.

CHROME
GOLD
BRONZE

*Illustrated:* **CLIMMA Vega** digital fain coil remote panel and infrared remote control.
The **CLIMMA Vega** digital control is supplied as option on CWS chilled water central systems ranging from 12,000 to 328,000 Btus/h and also for **CLIMMA** Cabin stand alone air-conditioners ranging from 4,000 to 22,000 Btus/h with electric heating function.

**VECO s.p.a. - Via Cantore, 6/8 20034 Giussano (MI) ITALY**
**Tel. +39 0362 35321 - fax. +39 0362 852995**
*E-mail:* info@veco.net
**www.veco.net**

CLIMMA air-conditioning is a high tech product, backed by an international service network and warranted by VECO, whose quality sistem is certified UNI EN ISO 9002 by DNV.

**CLIMMA®**
MARINE AIR CONDITIONING

# A1 *is your* **reliable solution** *for* **refit & repairs** *in* Greece

Sea Trade Marine Ltd and Yacht Agency International S.A., two of the oldest established yacht companies in Greece, who have between them more than 50 years experience in the yachting business, have recently been merged into A1 Yacht Trace Consortium, becoming Greece's leading yacht services organization.

Among its comprehensive range of services, A1 offers professional and reliable refit & repairs services in a number of shipyards, depending on the nature of your specific need. A1 will select and supervise, the most appropriate competent team of associated professionals, from qualified naval architects to experienced craftsmen, assuring that your yacht's needs, will be handled with outstanding care.

A1, the name you can trust for reliable repair & refit in Greece

Market Plan + Tsirigas

# A1
A1 YACHT TRADE CONSORTIUM

**RHODES:** Byronos 1 & Kanada St. 851 00 Rhodes, Greece, Tel.: +30 241 22927, Fax: +30 241 23393
**PIRAEUS:** 8, Akti Themistokleous, Zea Marina, 185 36 Piraeus, Greece, Tel.: +30 1 4511322, 4511334, Fax: +30 1 4523629

www.a1yachting.com  e-mail: a1@a1yachting.com

• *Rhodes* • *Piraeus* • *Corfu* • *Santorini* • *Mykonos* • *Cephalonia* • *Kalamata* • *Samos*

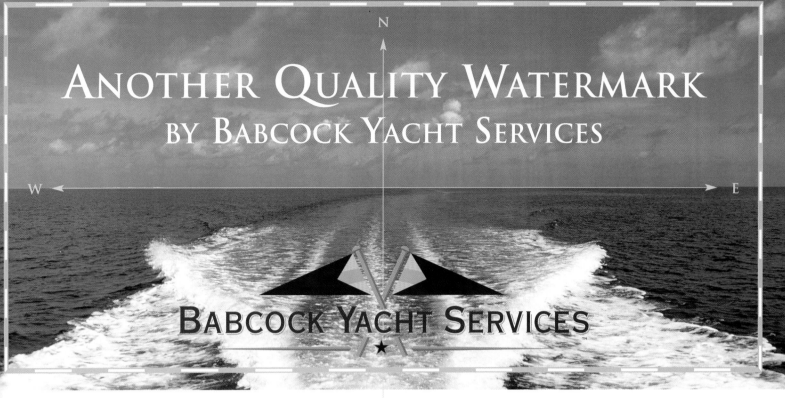

# ANOTHER QUALITY WATERMARK
## BY BABCOCK YACHT SERVICES

Specialists in superyacht refit, repair and design with a strong build capability. Located in Devonport, Auckland, New Zealand, Babcock Yacht Services is a division of New Zealand's largest ship and marine engineering organisation. Our extensive facilities and on site skill base are specifically geared to the specialist requirements of superyachts.

Facilities include: 181m dry-dock, 200t Syncrolift, 36m covered slipway, fully serviced alongside repair berths. Babcock Yacht Services can accommodate craft of up to 136m in length. Client references are available on request. Babcock Yacht Services, Queens Parade, Devonport, Auckland, New Zealand. Telephone (+64 9) 4461999.

www.babcockyachtservices.co.nz

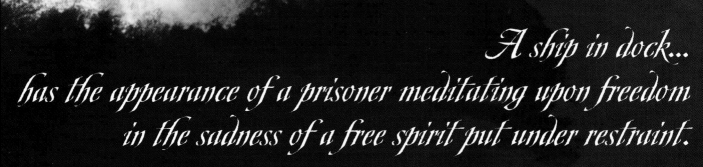

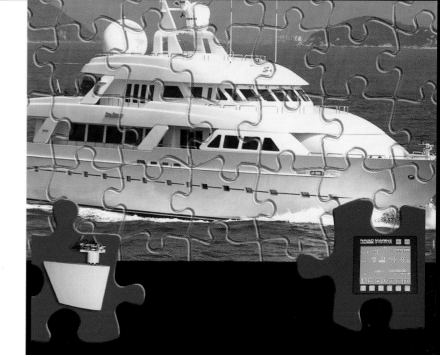

# THE
# YARDS

# Amels Holland

**Below:** the 62m (203ft) *Sarah*, with a Donald Starkey interior, under construction in Amels' dry dock at Makkum

Amels Holland traces its shipbuilding history as far back as 1917. However it has only seriously constructed and refitted large yachts since about 1982, although an experimental exercise at the yard some eight years earlier did see the launch of the 59m (193ft) *Altair*. The reason for the shift of interest to yacht building at that time was a response to increasing competition from Far Eastern shipyards. Nevertheless, diversification did not go entirely smoothly.

In fact Amels had managed to build seven significant motor yachts by 1987 when it finally succumbed to bankruptcy. That period saw the Amels family exit the scene and a variety of investors become involved. Indeed for a brief time the yard was picked up by high-profile American property developer Donald Trump, who bought into it because his then 86m (282ft) motor yacht *Trump Princess* (ex-*Nabila* and now *Kingdom 5KR*) had been refitted there. Trump's intention then was to use the yard to build *Trump Princess II*, a colossally ambitious project which he did actually get around to beginning, but in the end was forced to abandon early on after running into his own financial problems when recession hit America and subsequently most other major economies around the world. Indeed the impressive aluminium superstructure of that mighty project can still be seen on the Amels site today.

Since 1990, however, the yard has been owned by the Damen Shipyard Group, one of the largest shipbuilding operations in Europe, and has been on a

far more even keel. Managing a turnkey service from concept, design and engineering right through to final construction, as well as offering a full complement of refit, repair, refurbishment and maintenance services, Amels now boasts one of the best reputations in the world when it comes to the new builds and major refits of superyachts. Indeed since its first venture into yacht construction, the yard has so far delivered 17 significant motor yachts and refitted quite a few more. The Makkum yard's current scope is said to stretch from around 40m (131ft) up to around 120m (360ft), although the biggest launches to date have been the 70.5m (231ft) *Boadicea* in 1998 and the 75m (246ft) *Montkaj* in 1996. Intended to measure 128m (420ft), *Trump Princess II* would have actually proved something of a squeeze for the yard, had she been finished. Although Amels' dry dock is 130m (426ft)

long, the reality of modern beam and draught requirements would probably rule out anything quite that large again. However, Amels has recently acquired a second site in the south of the country which extends its options a little further. Following Damen's acquisition of the Royal Schelde shipyards in Vlissingen (Flushing), Amels has taken over one of the two facilities at the original yard, which has two covered dry docks of 145m (475ft) and 200m (656ft) respectively in the old Vlissingen harbour. Excluding the vast army of subcontracted specialists normally at work in the yard, Amels Holland currently employs 140 people at the Makkum site, which is located at the northernmost tip of the Ijsselmeer, and now a further 60 at Amels Schelde in Vlissingen. 'There is currently a fair degree of cross-fertilization between our two

facilities,' says the company's Commercial Director Frans Felix. 'At the moment employees formerly with Royal Schelde are up at Makkum undergoing training and so on and conversely we have experienced Makkum staff down in Vlissingen coordinating construction of the first of three new-build projects assigned to that facility.' Scheduled for delivery in September 2002, the first of these is the 61.5m (202ft) steel/aluminium motor yacht *Solemar*, styled inside and out by Mick Leach. 'All in all, Amels Holland has never been busier,' says Felix.

Since early May 2001 Amels has had no fewer than 11 new-build motor yacht projects under contract. These stretch from 46.5m (152ft) up to a record 93m (305ft). The first two to be delivered imminently during early summer 2001 are the 52m (171ft) *Toinie* and the 50m (164ft) *Kermit* – both styled by Terence Disdale.

**Above:** Donald Trump's 86m (282ft) *Trump Princess* (ex-*Nabila* and now *Kingdom 5KR*) is among several of the world's largest and most notable yachts to be refitted at Amels

**Top:** the 52m (171ft) *Toinie*, undergoing sea trials on the Ijsselmeer in May 2001

**Above:** the site at Makkum, where Amels currently employs a highly skilled workforce of 140 people

November 1999, she eventually left six months later after extensive renovation to her aft sections. As the requirement was to provide more aft deck area and garage space, her transom was cut off and a 3m (10ft) section was literally scarfed in aft of the engine room. By the end of the refit she had been lengthened to 78m (256ft). She also had her upper decks increased to give more overhead protection and a variety of new equipment installed.

Winter 1999/2000 saw the 1997 Codecasa 48.7m (160ft) *Renalo* at the yard for assorted modifications and maintenance. Other notable refits include former Amels' launches such as the 55m (180ft) *Lady Mona K* (ex-*Lady Ghislaine*) and the 56.7m (186ft) *Cleopatra-C* (ex-*My Gail III*). In April/May 2001, the Terence Disdale-designed 1997 Amels launch *Teddy* (ex-*Tigre d'Or*) was back at the yard for a minor refit. She was undergoing regular maintenance, incorporating the installation of new communications and entertainment systems and a complete repaint.

The most recent Amels new builds include the yard's second and slightly larger 52m (170ft) Terence Disdale-designed *Tigre d'Or* and the 50m (164ft) *Thunder Gulch*, both of which left the yard in 1999.

Besides the 2002 Vlissingen launch *Solemar*, there is also the 62m (203ft) Donald Starkey-styled *Sarah* which is due to be launched from Makkum in June 2002. No fewer than four more yachts are scheduled for delivery during 2003 – two 52m (170ft) projects and a 55m (180ft) vessel, all styled by the Terence Disdale studio, and one 72.2m (237ft) vessel with interior by Redman Whiteley Design. A further three more are scheduled for delivery in early summer 2004 – a 52m (171ft) styled by Cabinet Alberto Pinto, a 46.5m (152ft) from Donald Starkey and finally a 93m (305ft) with a 14.5m (48ft) beam and interior by Andrew Winch Designs, which in fact will be the biggest yacht the yard has ever built since *Montkaj*.

*Montkaj* herself was recently back at Amels for a major winter refit. Having arrived at the yard in

**AMELS HOLLAND**
PO Box 1, 8754 ZN Makkum
The Netherlands
Tel:+31 515 232525
Fax:+31 515 232719
E-mail: info@amels-holland.com

# Arredamenti Porto

Arredamenti Porto (AP) is not really a traditional shipyard but rather a company expressly oriented and organized for the repair, refit and refurbishment of large yachts over 40m (131ft) in length. Having been in business since 1987, it grew out of the wreckage of the old Fontana Arredamenti interior decoration and joinery company, which was well-known within the marine industry as a top quality interior subcontractor to a variety of major Italian boatbuilders.

The new company occupies the original Fontana

Arredamenti quayside premises in the old Port of Genoa, as well as a separate factory some 50km to the north in Ovada. In total the company directly employs 70 people, around 50 in its 2,000m² (21,520sqft) Genoa factory and 20 at its 5,000m² Ovada site, where it does much of its prefabrication and pre-mounting work which minimizes disruption on board. Today AP's workload is a 70:30 mix of both yacht and commercial ship refit and refurbishment work. On the commercial side it works primarily on cruise liners and fast ferries, the latter often requiring aeronautical-type ultralight interiors using special materials such as aluminium honeycomb. 'Over the past decade we have reduced the amount of work we do as a joinery subcontractor,' says the company's General Manager Matteo Costaguta, who joined AP in 1989 from the specialist ship, fast-ferry and yacht refit and repair yard in Campanella, Genoa. 'Now our only big OEM account is Perini Navi in Viareggio for which we have worked since 1994, building its extremely elegant interiors. But our primary focus is the large yacht refit side, where we act as main contractors, dealing directly with the owners or owners' representatives.'

The company's specialization is still very much top quality interior decoration and joinery work, including exterior work such as teak decks and rail cappings, but over the past 12 years it has expanded the range of services it has to offer. For example, one of the first things Costaguta did when he joined the company was to establish a technical department that could manage other work such as engineering, steelwork, dry docking and so forth. 'So the idea these days is that while AP clients are at the yard for changes to the interior, or deck replacement, the yard will also organize any other modification, maintenance and repair work,' says Costaguta. Indeed AP does not even require vessels to moor on its long deep-water quay outside its factory, where there are two berths capable of taking yachts up to 80m (262ft) in length. It can cope with boats either in the nearby new Marina Molo Vecchio, which caters for yachts up to 90m (295ft) on its quays and up to 60m (197ft) within the marina, or bigger yachts elsewhere in the various dry docks in the Port of Genoa, or even further afield in other ports or yards in Italy and beyond.

Over the years a host of owners of the world's biggest and finest superyachts have chosen AP, such is the company's reputation for the highest quality

**Main picture:** conveniently located not far from Portofino and the Riviera and only 10km from Genoa Airport, Arredamenti Porto specializes in high quality interior decoration and joinery work

**Above:** *Esmeralda*'s new traditional teak interior designed by Steve Howard

**Top:** *Shahnaz* looking resplendent moored alongside Arredamenti Porto's quay, after receiving a significant extension to her bridge deck (above)

interior and joinery work. To date the longest yacht that AP has worked on in the Port of Genoa was the classic 1931 Blohm & Voss 136m (446ft) *Savarona*, now the fourth longest private yacht in the world. She went to AP for recaulking and repair to her teak decks and for various interior modifications during 1997/98.

Two large jobs were in progress at AP until early summer 2001. The 54m (177ft) Dutch-built tug *Itasca*, converted to a yacht in 1980, came to AP for a completely new interior. She was scheduled to leave in June 2001. The 62.5m (205ft) steel Codecasa motor yacht *Esmeralda* was there until May 2001 for a new traditional teak interior and modified upper saloon, all designed by Steve Howard. During the same period, AP completed a new public deck area aboard the 200m (656ft) cruise liner *Costa Tropicale* which has been under refurbishment in Genoa.

Other recent big AP projects include the 38.25m (125ft) CRN motor yacht *Santa Cruz Tres*, which did not actually make the trip to Genoa but stayed at the Watershed yard in France where she was lengthened. There AP installed a completely new Michael Kirschstein-styled interior, relaid her teak decks, renewed her capping rails, installed a

new air-conditioning system and replaced all her insulation. She was completed in 2000.

In 1999/2000 AP reworked the whole interior of the 45.7m (149ft 8in) motor yacht *Istranka*, launched in Yugoslavia in 1952 as the presidential yacht. AP ministered to her during her rebuild at a yard in La Spezia (see previous article in the Refit Annual 2002). At the same time the 63m (207ft) *Shahnaz* (ex-*El Bravo*) was in the Port of Genoa. She came to AP for significant alterations requested by her new Middle Eastern owners. Her bridge deck was lengthened and the accommodation augmented to cater for an increase in the number of crew and security staff. By the time she left the yard she could hold over 60 people on board whereas previously she had the capacity to accommodate up to 40 in total.

Others notables among the many in for more routine refurbishment included the likes of the 63m (207ft) *Rosenkavalier*, 57.6m (189ft) *Princess Tanya*, the 43m (141ft) *Sanctuary*, the 62m (203ft) *Virginian* and many others for Mediterranean Yachts.

As regards business with Perini Navi, AP still supplies all the joinery work to what is the world's busiest builder of larger steel and aluminium sailing superyachts. The most recent launches were the 40m (131ft) ketch *Thetis* for which AP built the owner and guest areas and the 53m (174ft) A*tmosphere*, for which AP constructed the crew quarters.

# Arredamenti Porto

*Interiors and woodworks everywhere in Europe*

*General Refitting, drydocking and maintenance in Genoa*

*Ultralight interior technology and production*

# Devonport Yachts

**Below:** an impressive sight as the sailing yacht *Adix* enters one of the covered docks at Devonport while still fully masted

The sheer scale of Britain's three-century-old Devonport Royal Dockyard and the extent of its facilities along a 5km stretch of the River Tamar in Plymouth, Devon, leaves most first-time visitors overwhelmed. With its 11 massive dry docks capable of accommodating large ships, access to five fitting-out basins, a covered complex of three sizeable docks, all of which are able to house frigate-class warships, and over 45,000m² (484,200sqft) of factories and workshops catering to every technical marine need from the highest-quality yacht joinery to nuclear propulsion systems aboard submarines, Devonport is impressive by any standards.

Over 4,000 people work at the yard, which proudly claims not only to be the largest marine support complex in Europe, but also one that is totally self-contained and

vertically integrated in terms of engineering capability. Indeed when it comes to yachts there is no material or system specialization that it cannot accommodate.

The circumstances which provoked the formerly state-owned naval dockyard's push into the private sector developed during the mid-1980s. Around that time it was decided by the British government that the management of the Devonport Royal Dockyard – which along with Rosyth Royal Dockyard in Scotland looks after the maintenance of Britain's Royal Navy fleet – should be put out to tender. The idea was that with private sector management the yard could develop more efficiently and ultimately would win more and more non-military work. The winner was DML (Devonport Management Ltd), a company established specifically for the bid by three key investors: DML's ownership today comprises Halliburton/Brown & Root, with a controlling interest of 51 per cent, and Balfour Beatty and the Weir Group with 24.5

per cent each. DML managed the dockyard for a decade until 1997, when it finally purchased the yard outright. Devonport Yachts is a wholly-owned subsidiary of DML.

Still in the early stages of a £350 million modernization programme, the yard's turnover is now reported to be around £480 million, an increasing proportion of which is related to yachts. Over the past 15 years this well-financed yard has coped with vessels of all sizes down to as small as 15m (49ft), but its principal yacht business now involves new builds as well as major conversion and refit projects.

Capacity in Devonport's covered dock runs to around 145m (475ft). Certainly its catalogue of big yacht achievements makes impressive reading. For example, one of its earliest yacht projects was the refitting of *HMY Britannia* which, at 125.6m (412ft), remains one of the largest yachts to have visited the dockyard. Indeed at the time she was the third-largest private yacht in the world. Since then Devonport has gone on to complete

five more major refit projects for royal houses around the world. During *Britannia*'s final refurbishment before she was decommissioned in 1997, Devonport stripped out and restored all the royal suites, relaid around 23km of new, colour-matched, quarter-sawn teak deck planking, overhauled all machinery, stripped back her entire steel hull to bare metal for survey and repair and then refaired and repainted her.

Another milestone came in the early 1990s when the yard successfully won a contract to build the whole fleet of identical 20.4m (67ft) steel sloops for Chay Blyth's 1992/93 British Steel Challenge, a deal which contrasts well with *Britannia* and clearly illustrates the diversity of the yard's skills. That association with Blyth's Challenge Business not only continued with regular maintenance of the Challenge fleet, but also led to the yard being selected to build the replacement fleet for its Challenge 2000 race.

The 82.6m (270ft) classic steel twin-screw motor yacht

**Above:** with 11 dry docks, access to five fitting-out basins, over 4,000 employees and an annual turnover of £480 million, Devonport Royal Dockyard is the largest dockyard complex in Europe

**Right and below:** *Leander* is a regular visitor to the yard. Her most recent refit involved extensive engineering changes to bring her up to the latest MCA requirements, as well as two deck extensions fabricated from aluminium alloy

*Talitha G* also brought the yard much acclaim. Originally constructed by the Fr Krupp Germania Werft yard in 1929, she was so extensively refitted at Devonport over 1992 and 1993 that upon relaunch she qualified for a Lloyds' new ship classification certificate. Just about everything aboard was stripped bare and rebuilt, with a brand new interior designed by Jon Bannenberg.

During 1994 and 1995 the yard had the opportunity to demonstrate yet more versatility when it built the GRP-hulled *Lady Tiffany*. A modern 35m (115ft) motor yacht with an impressively spacious art deco interior, she ended up being voted one of the world's top five newly built yachts of 1995 by The Superyacht Society.

Over just 15 months during 1997 and 1998, Devonport undertook the transformation of a 30-year-old steel weather ship into the 2,000-ton, 74m (243ft) luxury motor yacht *Salem* for a Middle Eastern client. This project, the yard's most ambitious conversion to date, involved gutting the hull, installing replacement machinery and equipment, and building a new superstructure and accommodation.

Other regular superyacht visitors for refit and modification work include the likes of the 56m (184ft) *Southern Cross III*, the 62m (203ft) *Virginian* and the 75m (246ft) *Leander*. The yard also does regular refit work for the RNLI (Royal National Life-boat Institution) and is currently developing a new slipway-launched model that it hopes to start series building in the near future.

The current order book also looks very healthy, although little can be said of that, owing to the yard's policy on strict client and project confidentiality, a code that Devonport staff find particularly easy to abide by having spent so much of their working lives involved in Ministry of Defence projects and being bound by Britain's Official Secrets Act. However, the yard has disclosed that it currently has one new aluminium-hulled superyacht under construction, and rumour has it that it is a motor yacht of over 70m (230ft) in length, scheduled for delivery in the latter half of 2002.

**DEVONPORT YACHTS**
Devonport Royal Dockyard
Plymouth, PL1 4SG, UK
Tel:+44 (0)1752 323141
Fax:+44 (0)1752 323247
E-mail: david.semken@devonport.co.uk

# PRESTIGE INTERIORS

*Fine cabinetry built intelligently*

Prestige Interiors, 1951 Whitfield Park Drive, Sarasota, FL 34243, USA • Telephone: +1 941 751 6232

# Little Harbor Marine

**Below:** the 42.4m German Frers-designed ketch, *Rebecca*, received warranty work and repairs following an accident

Little Harbor Marine has been in business since 1985 on Aquidneck Island close to Newport, Rhode Island. Since its location is a former US Navy docking facility, it will come as no surprise that the yard is extremely well served in terms of access and infrastructure. Indeed off-season it now normally accommodates getting on for 200 pleasure boats of all sizes. 'Capacity within the yard is restricted to about 180 tonnes and a maximum draught of 4.9m (16ft),' says the General Manager Geoff Prior. However, in terms of length, the biggest yacht the yard could take undercover would be around 49m (160ft), although the ex-navy pier just outside can cater for much larger craft with draughts of up to at least 9m (30ft).

Yard facilities run to two Travelifts consisting of a 160-tonne and 40-tonne unit, but there will shortly be an additional 50-tonne lift. Little Harbor Marine continues to offer a comprehensive portfolio of services comprising everything from major refit projects and repairs to a wide range of routine maintenance programmes. Its expertise extends to both sail and power, although historically its reputation has been based rather more on its outstanding sailing yachts. Regardless of construction materials, Little Harbor Marine is renowned for being one of the best big yacht refitting and maintenance yards on the New England coast and consequently has an undeniably impressive client list. *Endeavour*, for example, which is one of the rebuilt classic J-Class America's Cup yachts, has been making regular calls to the yard for many years, in need of everything from repainting to more ambitious refitting or repair work. Built originally by Britain's Camper & Nicholsons in 1934 and subsequently reconstructed completely by the Royal Huisman Shipyard in Holland at the end of the 1980s for her previous owner Elizabeth Meyer, this simply stunning 39.6m (130ft) classic was brought back to Little Harbor Marine once again over the winter of 2000/2001

by her new owner. Having arrived towards the end of the North American season in September, she had her hull taken back to bare steel by high-pressure water-jetting. Any bad welds and seams were redone and various cuts were made into the hull to allow for repiping and assorted plumbing modifications. Her bilges were then repainted and eventually her hull was sponge-blasted, refaired and repainted with the *Endeavour* trademark dark blue from Awlgrip. All her teak decks were replaced and the doghouse and hatches were reconstructed with new glazing. Her classic panelled interior, the whole of which was redesigned by John Munford during the Dutch rebuild, was completely stripped out, revarnished and then put back.

Originally constructed in Germany by Abeking &

Rasmussen in 1988, *Extra Beat* is another regular visitor. Having arrived at the yard just before Christmas 2000, this 35.8m (117ft) German Frers-designed aluminium light-displacement sloop, which was originally built for Italian industrialist Gianni Agnelli as a daysailer, was most recently in for new teak decks, assorted external woodwork replacement and the reworking of the drive-train and thruster systems. Down below she had crew cabins for seven to eight installed along with a new galley, all to a scheme developed by Ted Hood Design in consultation with her crew.

There at the same time was *Palawan*, a 22.9m (75ft) Ted Hood-designed Little Harbor 75 which is a full-bodied GRP cruising sloop with centreboard. She arrived not only for her scheduled refit but also, as it happened, for major

repairs following a dismasting in the mid-Atlantic when she was actually on her way to the yard.

Going back a couple of years, the well-known 34.1m (112ft) steel-hulled sloops *Helios* and *Parsifal II* came in over consecutive summers of 1998 and 1999. Charter vessels, which were built originally by the Valdetarro yard, both left in time for the respective Antigua Charter Shows in 1999 and 2000. Having had all their engine room equipment extensively overhauled and new electronic systems added, both received new aft owners' cabins as well as modifications to their main saloons and galleys.

The 42.6m (139ft) Sparkman & Stephen-designed aluminium ketch *Sariyah*, with her John Munford interior, can frequently be found at Little Harbor Marine.

**Above:** located on a former US Navy docking site, Little Harbor Marine offers all the facilities to carry out extensive refit and maintenance programmes

**Above:** the most expensive refit project completed at the yard to date is the J-Class America's cup yacht *Endeavour*. Among the work done on her was a thorough overhaul of her mast and rigging (right)

Launched from Sensation Yachts in New Zealand back in 1994, the latest work done on her was a complete paint job and deck refurbishment, along with the installation of new batteries, chargers and inverters. The 42.4m (139ft) German Frers-designed aluminium ketch, *Rebecca*, which was built at Pendennis Shipyard in England in 1998, also went to the yard over the 1999/2000 winter for warranty work and repairs following an accident.

Technically, the most extensive refit that Little Harbor Marine has so far undertaken was five years ago. This was the *White Hawk* project, a classically-styled and cold-moulded Bruce King-designed 32m (105ft) ketch in need of a considerable rebuild. She was taken to the yard following a substantial fire, and among other things had her solid mahogany interior replaced.

The outside of the yard's pier has played host to bigger illustrious sailing yachts, among which are the mid-1990s 48.3m (158ft) Perini Navi steel and aluminium auxiliary ketches *Legacy* and *Morning Glory*. Both were recently alongside for routine works.

Little Harbor Marine is actually part of the 220-employee Ted Hood Company, which is owned by a group of low-profile investors who also happen to own the famous Hinckley yard located further up the New England coast at Southwest Harbor, Maine. The Ted Hood group consists of a variety of other related businesses, all of which occupy the same Little Harbor Landing site. Little Harbor Custom Yachts, for example, builds assorted custom projects comprising power and sail, and in the past has produced series-built models such as the Ted Hood-designed Little Harbor bluewater sailing yachts, WhisperJet express cruisers, Blackwatch sport fishing boats and others. Then there is the Little Harbor Yacht Brokerage and Little Harbor Charter Brokerage. And last, but by no means least, is the internationally renowned Ted Hood Design Group, which is always responsible for a significant number of sailboats being built all over the world and is on hand to help the Little Harbor engineering department with any design work.

**LITTLE HARBOR MARINE**
**1 Little Harbor Landing**
**Portsmouth, Rhode Island, USA**
**Tel:+1 401 683 7100**
**Fax:+1 401 683 7118**
**E-mail: inquiries@thco.com**

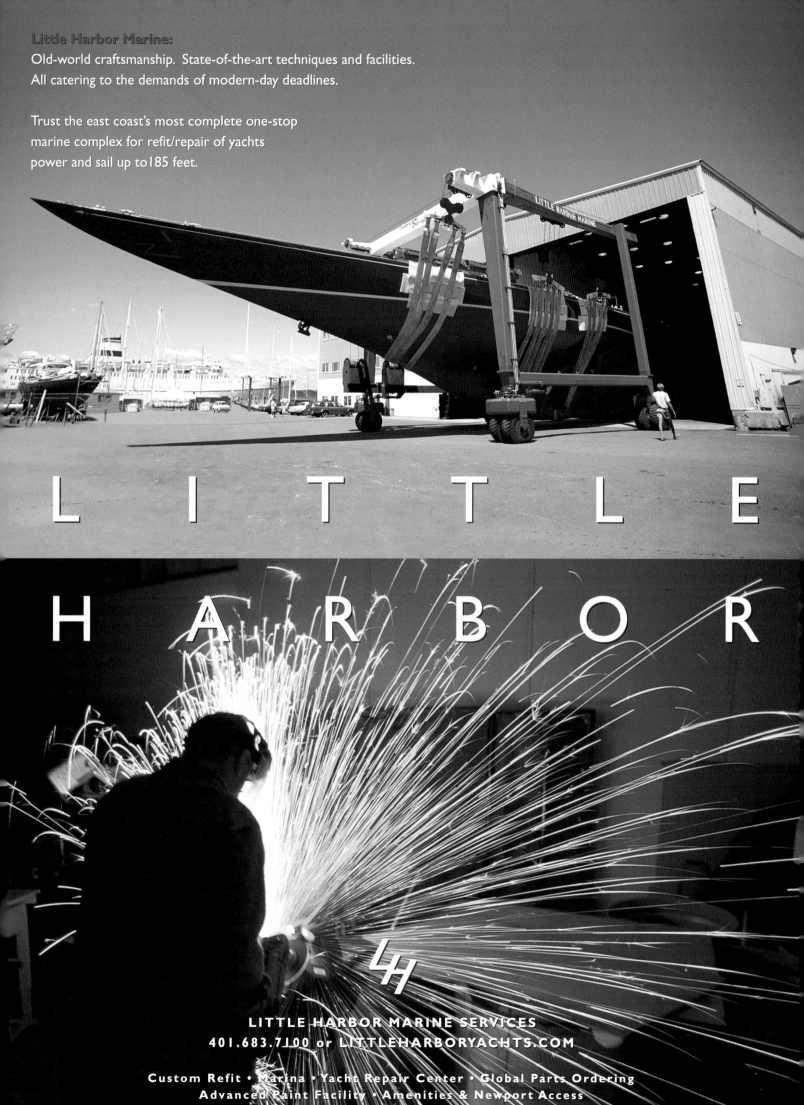

# die Oldenburger

MADE-TO-MEASURE EXCLUSIVE DESIGN

## THE FINE ART OF EXCLUSIVE YACHT INTERIORS

Oldenburger Möbelwerkstätten GmbH

Sanderstraße 21 · D - 49413 Dinklage/Germany

Fon: +49 (0)44 43/9 72-0 · Fax: +49 (0)44 43/9 72-2 75

E-mail: cad@oldenburger.com · Internet: www.oldenburger.com

# entertainment & electronics.

**Automatic Display / Cabinet Device**
(incl. autom. hinged door opener)

**Lifting Device for Camera**
(Non privat observation)

## harmony and function.

**Horizontal Display Device**
(shifting and turning)

**Display Pop Up Device**

**Device for Paintings**
(Display at support behind)

**Display Lifting Device**
(also in lifting / turnable
version available)

**Home+Marine Electronics**

28790 Schwanewede · Schützenplatz 12a · Tel. +49 (0) 421 66 15 46 · Fax +49 (0) 421 65 30 543 · e-Mail: info@home-marine.com

# It's the most beautiful things are
# made still more beautiful by us ...

Especially with Refit & Repair there is an above average level of
- very highly skilled crafts-manship
- finding solutions in con-junction with the customer and organisation
- reliability in keeping to the time schedule and flexibi-lity together with the tech-nological know-how which represents the qualities, distinguishing our Refit & Repair team. No challenge is to daunting and we offer you technological and visual solutions into the smallest details.

## metrica
### INTERIOR

BY RUDOLF RINCKLAKE VAN ENDERT

Bahnhofstr. 73 · D-48308 Senden · Tel. + 49 (0) 25 36 / 300 9-00 · Fax + 49 (0) 25 36 / 330 9-19

info@metrica.de · www.metrica-interior.com

# Robin Gates looks at the skills of
# Interior Refitters

**Top:** Loher's artisans demonstrate their skills at drafting, adding the finishing touches (centre) and selecting precious veneers (above)

**Right:** the craftsmanship of Loher Raumexclusiv is exemplified by this exquisite spa pool

The skills required of a superyacht interior refit company can be compared to those of a surgeon, since the new parts must not only work individually but also in concert, both aesthetically and functionally with what is retained from the pre-existing structure. Interior refit may be prompted by a change in yacht ownership, an expanding family, or shift in design taste. Alternatively, a long-lasting design may simply require renovation of faded and worn materials. Charter yachts, especially, require regular updating with the latest frills and fancies if they are to maintain their appeal. Whatever their motivation, interior designers are constantly pushing the boundaries of what is possible, calling for an increasingly broad spectrum of materials, many of which require novel expertise. A refit company may find itself ripping out baroque in favour of minimalist, or vice versa, while also negotiating ever more sophisticated systems for entertainments, air-conditioning, insulation and communications. Gone are the days when a multitude of sins could be glossed over with a fresh coat of varnish. Every cubic centimetre of volume is required to work. The surface design is only the finishing touch to a multi-layered complex structure as precisely engineered as the human body itself.

Many of the leading players in the field stretch back through several generations. German firm **Loher Raumexclusiv** has its roots in a small carpenter's shop opened by Karl Loher in 1931. In 1964, the shop was taken over and expanded by Alfred Loher who is now joined in the business of designing, building and installing interiors by sons Alfred junior and Roland. The family runs an extremely up-to-date company, equipped with the latest technology in all departments, from computer-aided design, through controlled environments for drying and preparing timber, to veneering, bonding, milling, inlay, and every kind of finishing from polished through gold leaf to specialist lacquers and gems. The firm began with residential and commercial interiors, and brought a wealth of expertise when it moved into aviation and yachting sectors. To ensure the highest quality, Loher maintains its own timber stocks sufficient for up to five years work, with a variety of grain patterns from the perfectly uniform to the intriguingly contorted patterns sliced from old roots. Loher combines wood with textiles, leathers and stone for interiors ranging from traditional to contemporary, and has the ability to handle every detail from custom doors to loose furniture and accessories. By training its own craftsmen, now numbering about 80, the firm ensures that its own high standards are maintained, while providing a complete service from draft sketch

to finished interior ready for occupation. The firm's key German representatives are based in Stuttgart, Frankfurt and Cologne, while export contracts have reached to Switzerland, Japan and Russia. Loher was certified in 1996 according to DIN ISO 9001 and stands for quality and innovation to the highest degree in every aspect.

For yachts making the classic passage between the Caribbean and Mediterranean seas, **Astilleros de Mallorca** could hardly be better placed. Situated within Palma harbour, at the eastern end of the Mediterranean, this yard routinely accommodates many of the largest superyachts afloat, with over a dozen undergoing all manner of refits at any one time. Yachts up to 70m (230ft) are handled by the four slips, while those staying afloat find over 250m (820ft) of well-serviced quays. Plastic tents cover yachts from end to end so that work can proceed independent of outside conditions, unconstrained by the fixed boundaries of a shed. The refit infrastructure is made up of specialist workshops for metalwork, machinery, carpentry, electrical systems and electronics, and dedicated design and technical offices. Astilleros de Mallorca is a real hive of refit industry, typically with around 200 subcontractors on site working alongside its own 60 employees, installing everything from new upholstery to

air-conditioning. The 52m (171ft) motor yacht *Jamaica Bay* was one of the yard's more recent refit visitors, returning to the oceans with a new spa pool on the sun deck, SOLAS safety upgrades and a superbly crafted traditional interior designed by Felix Buytendijk and built by De Ruiter Quality Interiors.

For some, a refit is not so much a job as an artistic mission. While the work of Florida-based cabinet and furniture builder **Prestige Interiors** has been impressing boat show visitors inspecting the new line of semi-custom motor yachts from Destiny Yachts, Prestige Interiors is also active in the refit market and enjoys working with some of the best interior designers in the world. Company leader Steve Halbrook, who has been in the yacht interior business for over three decades, neatly summarizes his company's approach when he says that, 'to produce a piece that exemplifies the designer's vision is a great source of pride. With their insight our work becomes art.' The company places great emphasis on detail, which not only pleases the customer but also keeps each job fresh for its 50 craftsmen and 15 support staff.

Computer techniques are playing an increasingly important role in the whole interior design and construction business, enhancing both speed and accuracy. **Yacht Interior Furnishings**, based in Fort Lauderdale, excels at building yacht furniture for refit projects and is equipped with the most capable computer-aided design, engineering and

manufacturing network, eliminating loose interpretation of what designers expect as a finished product. In-house furniture construction drawings are developed as three dimensional models, both providing a high level of precision for the cabinetry and simplifying the work of the cabinetmakers. Custom projects can benefit from the firm's nesting software, which enables cutting out parts automatically with an extremely accurate Computer

**Top:** craftsmen at Allan Revival put together a helm chair and sofa (above)

**Right and below right:** *Honey Money's* Violet Room displays the intricate details successfully executed by Struik & Hamerslag

Numeric Control (CNC) router. Yacht Interior Furnishings also offers a proprietary support service for yacht designers and builders, called Designers CAD Service, through which qualified design engineers with extensive experience in design of yacht furniture and a strong Computer Aided Design (CAD) background, convert customer supplied designs into construction drawings, and the company can manufacture the furniture too. Ultra-light cabinetry is a company forte, enabling significant enhancements to yacht performance without compromising structural integrity. The craftsmen are highly experienced in the application and matching of solid woods with a wide variety of veneers, using stains and tints to enhance or personalize woods where required. The more daring client might be tempted to investigate an extensive portfolio of exotic finishes.

Having been in the business since 1964, and constantly in demand, Dutch master **Struik & Hamerslag** possesses unsurpassed experience of yacht interiors and is frequently contracted for the most complex and challenging projects. The company employs around 170 specialized craftsmen in state-of-the-art workshops and can, quite literally, build anything a designer specifies. The firm's core activities are custom made joinery and furniture, and each item leaves the workshop complete for transport to the refit yard and installation. Struik & Hamerslag works with numerous collaborators in other areas, as shown by the extraordinary refit of the 43m (141ft) Diaship/Heesen motor yacht *Honey Money*. Following salt water and smoke damage resulting from a fire aboard an adjacent yacht, the owners requested an amazingly rich and ornate new interior from Donald Starkey Designs, revolving around the theme of honey and bees. Guest staterooms each have a different flower theme. There are electronically controlled screens, intricate inlays, fantastic lacquer finishes, electrically adjustable sofas, stairway murals, carbon-

fibre stair lighting and, to top it all, the work was finished within nine months to meet the owners' cruising schedule. Donald Starkey freely admits that no one but Struik & Hamerslag could have completed the project to such an impeccable standard within such a tight schedule. The company's capabilities extend to lightweight constructions, certified and fireproofing materials, and also renovation, by which a well-loved yacht interior is rejuvenated rather than redesigned. For example, the owner of *Trump Princess* requested that the yacht's original styling, colour schemes and materials be retained during refit, so Struik & Hamerslag searched worldwide for the necessary matching veneers, leathers and stones. For isolated damage, the firm's 'magicians' can also clean, repair and restore existing finishes on the spot, while giving surrounding artwork and precious materials the essential kid-glove treatment.

Repair and renovation poses its own particular problems, since the new must integrate seamlessly with the old if the result is not to resemble a patchwork quilt. **Allan Revival**, based in Majorca, is master of this meticulous art in which cigarette burns, scuffs and tears are rendered invisible. The technology was developed in the aviation

industry. James Allan established the company in 1996 as a mobile service for repairs to leathers and plastics, but as demand increased, so the portfolio of services expanded to include upholstery, and Allan Revival moved into new workshops, offices and showrooms where entire cabin and saloon interiors can be constructed. The company's craftsmen cover every aspect of interior refits, encompassing all soft furnishings, panelling, flooring, electrical installations, carpets, remote-controlled blinds and the repairs, fabric redyeing and specialist cleaning of renovation. Durable marine textiles, vinyls, leathers, acrylics and flooring are sourced worldwide, with a large selection held on display at the Santa Ponsa showrooms. Metalwork and carpentry services support the work of the firm's bilingual in-house designers. A typical project is the 40m (131ft) *Blue Attraction*, for which the master cabin and crew mess were refitted in Mallorca using suede panels, luxurious carpets, designer fabrics for all soft furnishings, and teak furniture accessories. Allan Revival also works in the South of France, Spain and Italy, and, in conjunction with Harris Grant Associates, has recently refitted seating areas for cinema studios aboard the 100m (328ft) motor yacht *Tatoosh* working in Cartagena, Gibraltar and Germany. Items may be prefabricated for installation overseas, and the craftsmen sometimes carry their own specialist sewing machines with them.

Founded in Italy in the 1920s, originally to furnish churches and colleges, **CeLI International Interiors,** one of world's leading manufacturers of high quality

joinery and custom-made interiors, also excels with the demanding art of dovetailing new work into established surroundings. The company focus fell on luxury yacht interiors in 1978, when Luciano Franceschini merged his own company with CeLI, and since that time a highly trained core of 50 workers has applied its skills to some outstanding projects. The architects and designers of the technical department use the latest CAD systems to guarantee a turnkey service, and the inter-disciplinary way of working enables solutions to the most taxing problems, using scale samples and prototypes to show exactly how things will turn out. In the joinery workshops, time-served hands and sophisticated machinery work with all types of wood construction, for panelling and

**Top:** among Allestimenti Tecnici Nautici's prestigious projects is the 36m motor yacht *Savannah* (above)

furniture, ranging from contemporary elegance to complex traditional forms. A dedicated metal-working department also handles mirrors and ceiling structures. By the time a piece leaves the assembly department, it is finished in every detail to conform exactly with its intended surroundings. A text book example of a CeLI interior refit is provided by the handsome 55m (180ft) CRN motor yacht *Shaf*, executed under refit designer Walter Franchini. Here, the upper and main decks were extensively refitted using Honduras mahogany for panelling, furniture and the mouldings of lacquered ceiling panels. Original soles and bulkheads, panelling, false ceilings, fixed furniture, doors and seating were dismantled, to be replaced with new work which was sensitively matched in terms of colour, finish and treatment to those materials retained in other areas. Computerized Numeric Control (CNC) machinery enabled perfect refitting.

Frequently, the construction and installation of a particular species of component, such as a door or a stairway, is the responsibility of a company which is permanently set up for such work. **Allestimenti Tecnici Nautici** can design and install complete interior decorations for any type of yacht, but this Italian firm is also known in all the best yards for manufacturing specialized marine equipment, ranging from hatches and ports to sliding saloon doors and watertight pantograph doors essential for the pilothouse and other exterior openings. Typical construction is based around 316 grade stainless steel, made to withstand the high seas environment. The company supplies many of the big

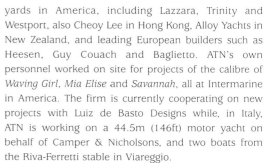

yards in America, including Lazzara, Trinity and Westport, also Cheoy Lee in Hong Kong, Alloy Yachts in New Zealand, and leading European builders such as Heesen, Guy Couach and Baglietto. ATN's own personnel worked on site for projects of the calibre of *Waving Girl*, *Mia Elise* and *Savannah*, all at Intermarine in America. The firm is currently cooperating on new projects with Luiz de Basto Designs while, in Italy, ATN is working on a 44.5m (146ft) motor yacht on behalf of Camper & Nicholsons, and two boats from the Riva-Ferretti stable in Viareggio.

Since being founded by Paul Birkley and Brian Gochoel in 1997, the American company **Belina Metal Works** has become established as an eminent manufacturer and installer of custom architectural metal components such as stairways and handrail systems, as well as lighting fixtures, tables and a variety of 'carry on' furniture. Belina Metal Works is part of the Belina Interiors group, which provides custom cabinetry, veneering and upholstering across the yacht building industry, and the company philosophy is, 'if it can be imagined, it can be built.' This is no idle boast, as demonstrated by recent projects in metal and wood which have realized the imaginations of top design firms such as A La Mar, Glade Johnson Design, Dee Robinson Design and Maxine Hoddinott Design. Belina Metal Works operates across America and Canada, and can also prefabricate items for shipment and installation in foreign yards. In 1999, the company moved into new, larger and comprehensively equipped premises in Tacoma, Washington. Most recently, it worked with Smith Bourne & Associates on the refit of the 52m (171ft) *Ice Bear* at Foss Shipyard in Seattle. The yacht was given a new look to suit her owners, to which end Belina Metal Works created and installed custom interior handrail systems, using ornamental panels and pewter-finished square stainless steel tubing, and both sides of a spiral staircase. Polished stainless steel rails were used for the exterior. The firm's ability to handle the twists and turns of building and fitting spiral stairways is also beautifully displayed aboard the Delta Marine motor yacht *Gallant Lady*. By carrying a wide range of stock hardware, from fiddles and handrails to self-contained, electrically-powered Hi-Low table pedestals, Belina Metal Works can help to fast track a refit requiring these essential items.

The dictionary's dry definition of refit is 'to make or become fit or serviceable again', but with companies such as these at work, the meaning goes far beyond serviceability.

# THE YARDS
# DIRECTORY

## ABEKING & RASMUSSEN SCHIFFS-UND YACHTWERF (GmbH & CO)

An der Fähre 2
27809 Lemwerder
Germany
Tel:+49 421 6733531
Fax:+49 421 6733115
Email: service@abeking.com

### YARD FACILITIES

| Type | Max length | Max beam | Max weight | Max draught |
|---|---|---|---|---|
| Syncrolift | 70m (230ft) | | 1,500t | 5m (16ft) |
| Crane | | | 8t | |
| Serviced quay space | 122m (400ft) | | | 7m (23ft) |

### SERVICES OFFERED

| Hull & structural work in: | Engineering | Fitting-out work | Exterior work | Exterior painting |
|---|---|---|---|---|
| Steel, aluminium, wood, composite plastics | Pipework, tanks, electrical & wiring, machinery overhaul & repair, shafts & propellers | Joinery, furnishings, interior finishing, electronics, TV, Satcom, sourcing/ supply of fittings | Bottom cleaning & painting, deck refinishing, woodwork, sanding & varnishing | Afloat in dry dock ashore under cover |

## ALPHA MARINE LTD

26 Skouse Street
185 36 Piraeus
Greece
Tel:+30 1 4280208
Fax:+30 1 4182136
Email: alphamrn@otenet.gr

### YARD FACILITIES

| Type | Max length | Max beam | Max weight | Max draught |
|---|---|---|---|---|
| Dry dock | 125m (410ft) | 22m (72ft) | | 6m (20ft) |
| Slipway | 75m (246ft) | | 1,000t | 4.5m (15ft) |
| Mobile lift | | | 300t | 4m (13ft) |
| Serviced quay space | 125m (410ft) | | | 6m (20ft) |

### SERVICES OFFERED

| Hull & structural work in: | Engineering | Fitting-out work | Exterior work | Exterior painting |
|---|---|---|---|---|
| Steel, aluminium, wood, composite plastics | Pipework, tanks electrical & wiring, machinery overhaul & repair, shafts & propellers | Joinery, furnishings, interior finishing, electronics, TV, Satcom, sourcing/ supply of fittings | Bottom cleaning & painting, deck refinishing, woodwork, sanding & varnishing | Afloat in dry dock ashore under cover |

## AMELS HOLLAND BV

PO Box 1
8754 ZN Makkum
The Netherlands
Tel:+31 515 232525
Fax:+31 515 232719
Email: info@amels-holland.com

### YARD FACILITIES

| Type | Max length | Max beam | Max weight | Max draught |
|---|---|---|---|---|
| Dry dock (under cover) | 120m (394ft) | 19m (62ft) | | 4m (13ft) |
| Crane | | | 60t | |
| Serviced quay space | 120m (394ft) | | | 4m (13ft) |

### SERVICES OFFERED

| Hull & structural work in: | Engineering | Fitting-out work | Exterior work | Exterior painting |
|---|---|---|---|---|
| Steel, aluminium | Pipework, tanks, electrical & wiring, machinery overhaul & repair, shafts & propellers | Joinery, furnishings interior finishing, electronics, TV, Satcom, sourcing/ supply of fittings | Bottom cleaning & painting, deck refinishing, woodwork sanding & varnishing | In covered dry dock |

## AMELS SCHELDE

PO Box 555
4380 AN Vlissingen
The Netherlands
Tel:+31 118 485000
Fax:+31 118 485050

### YARD FACILITIES

| Type | Max Length | Max beam | Max weight | Max draught |
|---|---|---|---|---|
| Dry dock (under cover) | 145m (475ft) | 20.5m (68ft) | | 5.80m (19ft) |
| Crane (2) | | | 50t | |
| Serviced quay space | 200m (656ft) | | | 5.80m (19ft) |

### SERVICES OFFERED

| Hull & structural work in: | Engineering | Fitting-out work | Exterior work | Exterior painting |
|---|---|---|---|---|
| Steel, aluminium | Pipeworks, tanks, electrical & wiring, machinery overhaul & repair, shafts & propellers | Joinery, furnishings, interior finishing, electronics, TV, Satcom, sourcing/supply of fittings | Bottom cleaning & painting, deck refinishing, woodwork sanding & varnishing | in covered dry dock |

## AMERICAN CUSTOM YACHTS INC

6800 SW Jack James Dr
Stuart
FL 34997, USA
Tel:+1 561 286 2835
Fax:+1 561 288 4147
Email: acy@6ate,net

### YARD FACILITIES

| Type | Max length | Max beam | Max weight | Max draught |
|------|-----------|----------|-----------|-------------|
| Dry dock | 119m (390ft) | 26m (85ft) | | 4m (13ft) |
| Slipway | 119m (390ft) | | 150t | 4m (13ft) |

### SERVICES OFFERED

| Hull & structural work in: | Engineering | Fitting-out work | Exterior work | Exterior painting |
|----------------------------|-------------|------------------|---------------|-------------------|
| Steel, aluminium, wood, composite plastics | Pipework, tanks, electrical & wiring, machinery overhaul & repair, shafts & propellers | Joinery, furnishings, interior finishing, electronics, TV, Satcom, sourcing/ supply of fittings | Bottom cleaning & painting, deck refinishing, woodwork, sanding & varnishing | Afloat in dry dock in covered dry dock |

## AMICO & CO SRL

Via Dei Pescatori
16129 Genova Porto
Italy
Tel:+39 010 247 0067
Fax:+39 010 247 0552
E-mail: amico.yard@pn.itnet.it

### YARD FACILITIES

| Type | Max length | Max beam | Max weight | Max draught |
|------|-----------|----------|-----------|-------------|
| Uncovered dry dock | 150m (492ft) | | | 9m (30ft) |
| Covered dry dock | 72m (236ft) | | | 9m (30ft) |
| Syncrolift | 40m (131ft) | | 200t | 9m (30ft) |
| Mobile lift | 45m (148ft) | | 320t | 11m (36ft) |
| Crane | | | 150t | |
| Serviced quay space | 110m (361ft) | | | 11m (36ft) |

### SERVICES OFFERED

| Hull & structural work in: | Engineering | Fitting-out work | Exterior work | Exterior painting |
|----------------------------|-------------|------------------|---------------|-------------------|
| Steel, aluminium, wood, composite plastics | Pipework, tanks, electrical & wiring, machinery overhaul & repair, shafts & propellers | Joinery, furnishings, interior finishing, electronics, TV, Satcom, sourcing/ supply of fittings | Bottom cleaning & painting, deck refinishing, woodwork, sanding & varnishing | Afloat in dry dock in covered dry-dock ashore under cover |

## ANTIGUA SLIPWAY LTD

PO Box 576
St John's
Antigua
Tel:+1 268 460 1056
Fax:+1 268 460 1566
Email: antslipway@candio.ag

### YARD FACILITIES

| Type | Max length | Max beam | Max weight | Max draught |
|------|-----------|----------|-----------|-------------|
| Slipway | 36m (120ft) | | 120t | 4m (13ft) |
| Mobile lift | 15m (50ft) | | 25t | 2m (7ft) |
| Serviced quay space | 60m (200ft) | | | 5m (16ft) |

### SERVICES OFFERED

| Hull & structural work in: | Engineering | Fitting-out work | Exterior work | Exterior painting |
|----------------------------|-------------|------------------|---------------|-------------------|
| Steel, aluminium, wood, composite plastics | Pipework, tanks, electrical & wiring, machinery overhaul & repair, shafts & propellers | Joinery, furnishings, interior finishing, electronics, TV, Satcom, sourcing/ supply of fittings | Bottom cleaning & painting, deck refinishing, woodwork, sanding & varnishing | Afloat |

## ARREDAMENTI PORTO SRL

Punta Molo Vecchio
16128 Genova
Italy
Tel:+39 010 277 0410
Fax:+39 010 246 1103
Email: info@arredementiporto.it

### YARD FACILITIES

| Type | Max length | Max beam | Max weight | Max draught |
|------|-----------|----------|-----------|-------------|
| Dry dock | 150m (492ft) | 20m (66ft) | | 6m (20ft) |
| Crane | | | 8t | |
| Serviced quay space | 200m (656ft) | | | 6m (20ft) |

### SERVICES OFFERED

| Hull & structural work in: | Engineering | Fitting-out work | Exterior work | Exterior painting |
|----------------------------|-------------|------------------|---------------|-------------------|
| Steel, aluminium | Pipework, tanks, electrical & wiring, machinery overhaul & repair, shafts & propellers | Joinery, furnishings, interior finishing, electronics, TV, Satcom, sourcing/ supply of fittings | Bottom cleaning & painting, deck refinishing, woodwork, sanding & varnishing | Afloat in dry dock in covered dry dock |

## ASTILLEROS DE MALLORCA

Contramuelle Mollet 11
07012 Palma de Mallorca
Baleares
Spain
Tel:+34 971 710645
Fax:+34 971 721368
Email: astillerosmallorca@logiccontrol.es

### YARD FACILITIES

| Type | Max Length | Max beam | Max weight | Max draught |
|------|-----------|----------|-----------|-------------|
| Slipway | 70m (230ft) | | 1,700t | 5.5m (18ft) |
| Crane | | | 20t | |
| Serviced quay space | 110m (360ft) | | | 8m (26ft) |

### SERVICES OFFERED

| Hull & structural work in: | Engineering | Fitting-out work | Exterior work | Exterior painting |
|---------------------------|-------------|------------------|---------------|-------------------|
| Steel, aluminium, wood, composite plastics | Pipework, tanks electrical & wiring, machinery overhaul & repair, shafts & propellers | Joinery, furnishings, interior finishing, electronics, TV, Satcom, sourcing/ supply of fittings | Bottom cleaning & painting, deck refinishing, woodwork, sanding & varnishing | Afloat |

## ASTILLEROS PALMA SL

Muelle Viejo, s/n
Espigon de la Consigna
07012 Palma de Mallorca
Baleares
Spain
Tel:+34 971 712303
Fax:+34 971 712802
Email: astipal@apdo.com

### YARD FACILITIES

| Type | Max length | Max beam | Max weight | Max draught |
|------|-----------|----------|-----------|-------------|
| Mobile lift | 40m (131ft) | | 150t | 5.5m (18ft) |
| Crane | | | 100t | |
| Serviced quay space | 60m (197ft) | | | 6m (20ft) |

### SERVICES OFFERED

| Hull & structural work in: | Engineering | Fitting-out work | Exterior work | Exterior painting |
|---------------------------|-------------|------------------|---------------|-------------------|
| Steel, aluminium, wood, composite plastics | Pipework, tanks, electrical & wiring, machinery overhaul & repair, shafts & propellers | Joinery, furnishings, interior finishing, sourcing/ supply of fittings | Bottom cleaning & painting, deck refinishing, woodwork, sanding & varnishing | Afloat in dry dock ashore under cover |

## ASTILLEROS Y VARADEROS 'EL RODEO'

Ctra Acceso Sur al Puerto de Algeciras, s/n
Algeciras (Cadiz)
Spain
Tel:+34 956 600511
Fax:+34 956 600431
Email: elrodeo@ cherrytel.com

### YARD FACILITIES

| Type | Max length | Max beam | Max weight | Max draught |
|------|-----------|----------|-----------|-------------|
| Slipway | 70m (230ft) | | 700t | 4m (13ft) |
| Crane | | | 2t | |
| Serviced quay space | 20m (65ft) | | | 3m (10ft) |

### SERVICES OFFERED

| Hull & structural work in: | Engineering | Fitting-out work | Exterior work | Exterior painting |
|---------------------------|-------------|------------------|---------------|-------------------|
| Steel, aluminium, wood, composite plastics | Pipework, tanks, electrical & wiring, machinery overhaul & repair, shafts & propellers | Joinery, furnishings, interior finishing, electronics, TV, Satcom, sourcing/ supply of fittings | Bottom cleaning & painting, deck refinishing, woodwork, sanding & varnishing | Afloat in dry dock in covered dry dock ashore under cover |

## ATLANTIC DRY DOCK CORPORATION

8500 Heckscher Drive
Jacksonville
Florida 32226
USA
Tel:+1 904 251 1545
Fax:+1 904 251 3500
Email: jaxsales@atlanticmarine.com

### YARD FACILITIES

| Type | Max Length | Max beam | Max weight | Max draught |
|------|-----------|----------|-----------|-------------|
| Dry dock | 189m (620ft) | 28m (93ft) | | 9m (30ft) |
| Slipway | 91m (300ft) | | 22m (72ft) | 5m (17ft) |
| Syncrolift | | | | |
| Crane | | | 150t | |
| Serviced quay | 396m (1,300ft) | | | 5m (17ft) |

### SERVICES OFFERED

| Hull & structural work in: | Engineering | Fitting-out work | Exterior work | Exterior painting |
|---------------------------|-------------|------------------|---------------|-------------------|
| Steel, aluminium, composite plastics | Pipework, tanks, electrical & wiring | | | |

## BABCOCK INTERNATIONAL GROUP PLC

Facilities Management Division
Rosyth Royal Dockyard
Rosyth
Fife KY11 2YD
UK
Tel:+44 (0)1383 422629
Fax:+44 (0)1383 423182

### YARD FACILITIES

| Type | Max length | Max beam | Max weight | Max draught |
|------|-----------|----------|-----------|-------------|
| Dry dock | 310m (1,017ft) | 31.4m (103ft) | | 11.0m (36ft) |
| Syncrolift | 73m (240ft) | | 1,700t | |
| Serviced quay space | 250m (820ft) | | | 11.0m (36ft) |

### SERVICES OFFERED

| Hull & structural work in: | Engineering | Fitting-out work | Exterior work | Exterior painting |
|----------------------------|-------------|------------------|---------------|-------------------|
| Steel, aluminium, wood, composite plastics | Pipework, tanks, electrical & wiring, machinery overhaul & repair, shafts & propellers | Joinery, furnishings, interior finishing, electronics, TV, Satcom, sourcing/ supply of fittings | Bottom cleaning & painting, deck refinishing, woodwork, sanding & varnishing | Afloat ashore under cover |

## BERTHON BOAT CO LTD

The Shipyard
Lymington
Hampshire SO41 3YL
UK
Tel:+44 (0)1590 673312
Fax:+44 (0)1590 676353
Email: brokers@berthon.co.uk

### YARD FACILITIES

| Type | Max length | Max beam | Max weight | Max draught |
|------|-----------|----------|-----------|-------------|
| Slipway | 30m (100ft) | | 100t | 4.5m (15ft) |
| Mobile lift | 25m (80ft) | | 45t | 4.5m (15ft) |
| Crane | | | 1.5t | |
| Serviced quay space | 45m (150ft) | | | 4.5m(15ft) |

### SERVICES OFFERED

| Hull & structural work in: | Engineering | Fitting-out work | Exterior work | Exterior painting |
|----------------------------|-------------|------------------|---------------|-------------------|
| Steel, aluminium, wood, composite plastics | Pipework, tanks, electrical & wiring, machinery overhaul & repair, shafts & propellers | Joinery, furnishings, interior finishing, electronics, TV, Satcom, sourcing/ supply of fittings | Bottom cleaning & painting, deck refinishing, woodwork, sanding & varnishing | Ashore under cover |

## RICHARD BERTRAM, INC YACHT

3550 NW 21st Street
Miami
FL 33142
USA
Tel:+1 305-633-9761
Fax:+1 305-634-3107
Email: serviceyard@bertramyacht.com

### YARD FACILITIES

| Type | Max length | Max beam | Max weight | Max draught |
|------|-----------|----------|-----------|-------------|
| Syncrolift | 30m (100ft) | | 100t | 2.5m (8ft) |
| Crane | | | 2t | |
| Serviced quay space | 30m (100ft) | | | 2.5m (8ft) |

### SERVICES OFFERED

| Hull & structural work in: | Engineering | Fitting-out work | Exterior work | Exterior painting |
|----------------------------|-------------|------------------|---------------|-------------------|
| Steel, aluminium, composite plastics | Pipework, tanks, electrical & wiring, machinery overhaul & repair, shafts & propellers | Joinery, furnishings, interior finishing, electronics, TV, Satcom, sourcing/ supply of fitting | Bottom cleaning & painting, deck refinishing, woodwork, sanding & varnishing | Afloat in dry dock in covered dry dock ashore under cover |

## BEZZINA SHIP REPAIR YARD LTD

19-24 Coal Wharf
Marsa PLA 08
Malta
Tel:+356 829 091
Fax:+356 809 719

### YARD FACILITIES

| Type | Max length | Max beam | Max weight | Max draught |
|------|-----------|----------|-----------|-------------|
| Dry dock | 140m (460ft) | 24.5m (80ft) | | 4.75m (15ft) |
| Mobile lift | | | 30t | 5m (16ft) |
| Serviced quay space | 130m (426ft) | | | 10m (33ft) |

### SERVICES OFFERED

| Hull & structural work in: | Engineering | Fitting-out work | Exterior work | Exterior painting |
|----------------------------|-------------|------------------|---------------|-------------------|
| Steel, aluminium, wood | Pipework, tanks, electrical & wiring, machinery overhaul & repair, shafts & propellers | Joinery | Bottom cleaning & painting, deck refinishing, woodwork, sanding & varnishing | Afloat in covered dry dock |

## BLOHM + VOSS REPAIR GmbH

Hermann Blohm Strasse 2
20457 Hamburg
Germany
Tel:+49 40 3119 8000
Fax:+49 40 3119 3305
Email: BVrepair@blohmvoss.thyssen.com

### YARD FACILITIES

| Type | Max length | Max beam | Max weight | Max draught |
|------|-----------|----------|-----------|-------------|
| Dry dock | 351.2m (1,152ft) | 59.2m (194ft) | | 9.45m (31ft) |
| Crane | | | 50t | |
| Serviced quay space | 400m (1,312ft) | | | 10m (33ft) |

### SERVICES OFFERED

| Hull & structural work in: | Engineering | Fitting-out work | Exterior work | Exterior painting |
|---------------------------|-------------|------------------|---------------|-------------------|
| Steel, aluminium | Pipework, tanks, electrical & wiring, machinery overhaul & repair, shafts & propellers | Joinery, furnishings, interior finishing, electronics, TV, Satcom, sourcing/ supply of fittings | Bottom cleaning & painting, deck refinishing, woodwork, sanding & varnishing | Afloat in dry dock in covered dry dock ashore under cover |

## BOAT YARD PALMA

Muelle Viejo s/n
EDIF OTP 07012 Palma de Mallorca
Beleares
Spain
Tel:+34 971 718302
Fax:+34 971 718611
Email: boatyardpalma@redestb.es

### YARD FACILITIES

| Type | Max length | Max beam | Max weight | Max draught |
|------|-----------|----------|-----------|-------------|
| Mobile lift | 37m (121ft) | | 150t | 5m (16ft) |
| Serviced quay space | 65m (213ft) | | | 6m (20ft) |

### SERVICES OFFERED

| Hull & structural work in: | Engineering | Fitting-out work | Exterior work | Exterior painting |
|---------------------------|-------------|------------------|---------------|-------------------|
| Steel, aluminium, wood, composite plastics | Pipework, tanks, electrical & wiring, machinery overhaul & repair, shafts & propellers | Joinery, furnishings, interior finishing, electronics, TV, Satcom, sourcing/ supply of fittings | Bottom cleaning & painting, deck refinishing, woodwork, sanding & varnishing | Afloat ashore under cover |

## BRADFORD MARINE

3051 State Road 84
Fort Lauderdale
FL 33312, Florida
USA
Tel:+1 954 791 3800
Fax:+1 954 583 9938

### YARD FACILITIES

| Type | Max length | Max beam | Max weight | Max draught |
|------|-----------|----------|-----------|-------------|
| Syncrolift | 46m (150ft) | | 300t | 3m (10ft) |
| Crane | | | 15t | |
| Serviced quay space | 52m (170ft) | | | 3m (10ft) |

### SERVICES OFFERED

| Hull & structural work in: | Engineering | Fitting-out work | Exterior work | Exterior painting |
|---------------------------|-------------|------------------|---------------|-------------------|
| Steel, aluminium, wood, composite plastics | Pipework, tanks, electrical & wiring, machinery overhaul & repair, shafts & propellers | Joinery, furnishings, interior finishing, electronics, TV, Satcom, sourcing/ supply of fittings | Bottom cleaning & painting, deck refinishing, woodwork, sanding & varnishing | Afloat |

## CRN SHIPYARD, ANCONA

Via Mattei 26
60125 Ancona
Italy
Tel:+39 071 201754
Fax:+39 071 200008
Email: info@crn-yacht.com

### YARD FACILITIES

| Type | Max length | Max beam | Max weight | Max draught |
|------|-----------|----------|-----------|-------------|
| Dry dock | 85m (279ft) | 15m (49ft) | | 4m (13ft) |
| Slipway | 80m (262ft | | 1,000t | 5m (16ft) |
| Mobile lift | 25m (82ft) | | 100t | 5m (16ft) |
| Crane | | | 20t | |
| Serviced quay space | 82m (269ft) | | | 4.5m (15ft) |

### SERVICES OFFERED

| Hull & structural work in: | Engineering | Fitting-out work | Exterior work | Exterior painting |
|---------------------------|-------------|------------------|---------------|-------------------|
| Steel, aluminium, wood, composite plastics | Pipework, tanks, electrical & wiring, machinery overhaul & repair, shafts & propellers | Joinery, furnishings, interior finishing, electronics, TV, Satcom, sourcing/ supply of fittings | Bottom cleaning & painting, deck refinishing, woodwork, sanding & varnishing | Ashore under cover |

## CABLE MARINE INC

2491 Sth Rd 84
1517 SE 16th Street
Fort Lauderdale
FL 33315, Florida
USA
Tel:+1 954 587 4000
Fax:+1 954-587 4017

### YARD FACILITIES

| Type | Max length | Max beam | Max weight | Max draught |
|---|---|---|---|---|
| Slipway | 37m (120ft) | | | 3m (10ft) |

### SERVICES OFFERED

| Hull & structural work in: | Engineering | Fitting-out work | Exterior work | Exterior painting |
|---|---|---|---|---|
| Steel, aluminium, composite plastics | | Joinery, furnishings, interior finishing, sourcing/ supply of fittings | Bottom cleaning & painting, deck refinishing, woodwork, sanding & varnishing | Afloat in covered dry dock |

## CAIRNS SLIPWAY

PO Box 5000
Cairns 4870
Queensland, Australia
Tel:+61 740 527354
Fax:+61 740 352332
Email: nqea-cns@nqea.com.au

### YARD FACILITIES

| Type | Max length | Max beam | Max weight | Max draught |
|---|---|---|---|---|
| Dry dock | 60m (197ft) | 11m (36ft) | | 3m (10ft) |
| Slipway | 75m (246ft) | | 1.500t | 5m (16ft) |
| Crane | | | 70t | |
| Serviced quay space | 75m (246ft) | | | 5m (16ft) |

### SERVICES OFFERED

| Hull & structural work in: | Engineering | Fitting-out work | Exterior work | Exterior painting |
|---|---|---|---|---|
| Steel, aluminium, wood, composite plastics | Pipework, tanks, electrical & wiring, machinery overhaul & repair, shafts & propellers | Joinery, furnishings, interior finishing, electronics, TV, Satcom, sourcing/ supply of fittings | Bottom cleaning & painting, deck refinishing, woodwork, sanding & varnishing | Afloat in dry dock in covered dry dock ashore under cover luxury paint finishes |

## CAMMELL LAIRD (GIBRALTAR)

PO Box 858
Main Wharf Road
Gibraltar
Tel:+350 59400/40354
Fax:+350 44404
Email: mail@lairds.gi

### YARD FACILITIES

| Type | Max length | Max beam | Max weight | Max draught |
|---|---|---|---|---|
| Dry docks (3) | 270m (886ft) | 38m (125ft) | | 11m (36ft) |
| Crane | | | 45t | |
| Serviced quay space | 800m (2625ft) | | | 11m (36ft) |

### SERVICES OFFERED

| Hull & structural work in: | Engineering | Fitting-out work | Exterior work | Exterior painting |
|---|---|---|---|---|
| Steel, aluminium | Pipework, tanks, electrical & wiring, machinery overhaul & repair, shafts & propellers | Joinery, furnishings, interior finishing, electronics, TV, Satcom, sourcing/ supply of fittings | Bottom cleaning & painting, deck refinishing, woodwork, sanding & varnishing | Afloat in dry dock in covered dry dock |

## CAMPBELL INDUSTRIES

PO Box 121870
San Diego
California CA 92112 – 1870, USA
(8th Avenue at Harbor Drive, San Diego CA 92101)
Tel:+1 619 233 7115
Fax:+1 619 233 5259
Email: kampbell@inetworld.net

### YARD FACILITIES

| Type | Max length | Max beam | Max weight | Max draught |
|---|---|---|---|---|
| Dry dock | 118m (387ft) | 17.6m (58ft) | | 6.4m (21ft) |
| Slipway | 49m (160ft) | | 550t | |
| Crane | | | 50t | |
| Serviced quay space | 150m (492ft) | | | 7.6m (25ft) |

### SERVICES OFFERED

| Hull & structural work in: | Engineering | Fitting-out work | Exterior work | Exterior painting |
|---|---|---|---|---|
| Steel, aluminium, wood, composite plastics | Pipework, electrical & wiring, machinery overhaul & repair, shafts & propellers | Joinery, furnishings, interior finishing, electronics, TV, Satcom, sourcing/ supply of fittings | Bottom cleaning & painting, deck refinishing, woodwork, sanding & varnishing | In dry dock in covered dry dock ashore under cover |

## CAMPER & NICHOLSONS (YACHTS) LTD

Mumby Road
Gosport
Hants PO12 1AH
UK
Tel:+44 (0)23 92580221
Fax:+44 (0)23 92501882
Email: design@cnyachts.co.uk

### YARD FACILITIES

| Type | Max length | Max beam | Max weight | Max draught |
|------|-----------|----------|-----------|-------------|
| Mobile lift | | | 180t | 4.9m (16ft) |
| Crane | | | 200t | |

### SERVICES OFFERED

| Hull & structural work in: | Engineering | Fitting-out work | Exterior work | Exterior painting |
|---------------------------|-------------|------------------|---------------|-------------------|
| Steel, aluminium, wood, composite plastics | Pipework, tanks, electrical & wiring, machinery overhaul & repair, shafts & propellers | Joinery, furnishings, interior finishing, electronics, TV, Satcom, sourcing/ supply of fittings | Bottom cleaning & painting, deck refinishing, woodwork, sanding & varnishing | Ashore under cover |

## CANTIERE NAVALE RIVIERA SRL

Portosole Molo Est
18038 Sanremo
Italy
Tel:+39 0184 505117
Fax:+39 0184 574474
Email: cnriv@tlscallnet.it

### YARD FACILITIES

| Type | Max Length | Max beam | Max weight | Max draught |
|------|-----------|----------|-----------|-------------|
| Syncrolift | 60m (197ft) | | 700t | 5m (16ft) |
| Crane | | | 45t | |
| Serviced quay space | | | | |

### SERVICES OFFERED

| Hull & structural work in: | Engineering | Fitting-out work | Exterior work | Exterior painting |
|---------------------------|-------------|------------------|---------------|-------------------|
| Steel, aluminium, wood | Pipework, tanks, electrical & wiring, machinery overhaul & repair, shafts & propellers | Joinery, furnishings, interior finishing, electronics, TV, Satcom, sourcing/supply of fittings | Bottom cleaning & painting, deck refinishing, woodwork, sanding & varnishing | Afloat in dry dock ashore under cover |

## CANTIERE NAVALI DELL' ARGENTARIO SRL

Localita Vallo
58019 Porto S Stefano
Italy
Tel:+39 0564 814115
Fax:+39 0564 817202
Email: cnargen@tin.it

### YARD FACILITIES

| Type | Max length | Max beam | Max weight | Max draught |
|------|-----------|----------|-----------|-------------|
| Dry dock | 40m (131ft) | 8.5m (28ft) | | 4.5m (15ft) |
| Slipway | 40m (131ft) | | 400t | 4.5m (15ft) |
| Crane | | | 25t | |
| Serviced quay space | 40m (131ft) | | | 4.5m (15ft) |

### SERVICES OFFERED

| Hull & structural work in: | Engineering | Fitting-out work | Exterior Work | Exterior painting |
|---------------------------|-------------|------------------|---------------|-------------------|
| Steel, aluminium, wood, composite plastics | Pipework, tanks, electrical & wiring, machinery overhaul & repair, shafts & propellers | Joinery, furnishings, interior finishing, electronics, TV, Satcom, sourcing/ supply of fittings | Bottom cleaning & painting, deck refinishing, woodwork, sanding & varnishing | Afloat in dry dock ashore under cover |

## CANTIERI NAVALI BECONCINI SRL

Viale S Bartolomeo 428
La Spezia
Italy, Cap 19138
Tel:+39 0187 524127
Fax:+39 0187 524136
Email: beconciniShipyard@tin.it

### YARD FACILITIES

| Type | Max length | Max beam | Max weight | Max draught |
|------|-----------|----------|-----------|-------------|
| Mobile lift | 40m (131ft) | | 280t | 6m (20ft) |
| Crane | | | | |

### SERVICES OFFERED

| Hull & structural work in: | Engineering | Fitting-out work | Exterior work | Exterior painting |
|---------------------------|-------------|------------------|---------------|-------------------|
| Steel, aluminium, wood | Pipework, tanks, electrical & wiring, machinery overhaul & repair, shafts & propellers | Joinery, interior finishing, furnishings, supply of fittings | Bottom cleaning & painting, deck refinishing, woodwork, sanding & varnishing | Afloat in covered dry dock ashore under cover |

## CHANTIER NAVAL RODRIGUEZ

Port Camille Rayon
06220 Golfe Juan
France
Tel:+33 493 630 697
Fax:+33 493 630 638

### YARD FACILITIES

| Type | Max length | Max beam | Max weight | Max draught |
|---|---|---|---|---|
| Mobile lift | 35m (115ft) | | 100t | 3m (10ft) |
| Crane | | | 20t | |
| Serviced quay space | 30m (100ft) | | | 5m (16ft) |

### SERVICES OFFERED

| Hull & structural work in: | Engineering | Fitting-out work | Exterior work | Exterior painting |
|---|---|---|---|---|
| Steel, aluminium, wood, composite plastics | Tanks, electrical & wiring, machinery overhaul & repair, shafts & propellers | Electronics, TV, Satcom, sourcing/ supply of fittings | Bottom cleaning & painting, deck refinishing, woodwork, sanding & varnishing | Ashore under cover |

## CHINNOCK MARINE INC

518 West Las Olas Boulevard
Fort Lauderdale
FL 33312, USA
Tel:+1 954 763 2250
Fax:+1 954 763 2294
Email: chinnock@chinnock.com

### YARD FACILITIES

| Type | Max length | Max beam | Max weight | Max draught |
|---|---|---|---|---|
| Mobile lift | 26.5m (87ft) | 7m (23ft) | 70t | 3.3m (11ft) |
| Crane | | | 18t | |
| Serviced quay space | 33.5m (110ft) | | | 2.7m (9ft) |

### SERVICES OFFERED

| Hull & structural work in: | Engineering | Fitting-out work | Exterior work | Exterior painting |
|---|---|---|---|---|
| Steel, aluminium, wood, composite plastics | Pipework, tanks, electrical & wiring, machinery overhaul & repair, shafts & propellers | Joinery, furnishings, interior finishing, electronics, TV, Satcom, sourcing/ supply of fittings | Bottom cleaning & painting, deck refinishing, woodwork, sanding & varnishing | Afloat ashore under cover |

## CODECASADUE SpA

Via Trieste 3/7
Viareggio
Italy
Tel:+39 0584 383945
Fax:+39 0584 388076
Email: info@codecasayachts.com

### YARD FACILITIES

| Type | Max length | Max beam | Max weight | Max draught |
|---|---|---|---|---|
| Slipway | 42m (138ft) | | 200/500t | 3m (10ft) |
| Mobile lift | 35m (115ft) | | 150t | 3m (10ft) |
| Crane | | | 5t | |
| Serviced quay space | 35m (115ft) | | | 3m (10ft) |

### SERVICES OFFERED

| Hull & structural work in: | Engineering | Fitting-out work | Exterior work | Exterior painting |
|---|---|---|---|---|
| Steel, aluminium, wood, composite plastics | Pipework, tanks, electrical & wiring, machinery overhaul & repair, shafts & propellers | Joinery, furnishings, interior finishing, electronics, TV, Satcom, sourcing/ supply of fittings | Bottom cleaning & painting, deck refinishing, woodwork, sanding & varnishing | Afloat ashore under cover |

## COLONNA YACHTS

2401 Kimball Terrace
Norfolk, Virginia
USA 23504
Tel:+1 757 627 0737
Fax:+1 757 627 5562
Email: colonna@series2000.com

### YARD FACILITIES

| Type | Max length | Max beam | Max weight | Max draught |
|---|---|---|---|---|
| Slipway | 64m (210ft) | | 1,200t | 4.3m (14ft) |
| Syncrolift | 64m (210ft) | | 1,000t | 5.5m (18ft) |
| Crane | | | 90t | |
| Serviced quay space | 100m (320ft) | | | 5.5m (18ft) |

### SERVICES OFFERED

| Hull & structural work in: | Engineering | Fitting-out work | Exterior work | Exterior painting |
|---|---|---|---|---|
| Steel, aluminium, wood, composite plastics | Pipework, tanks, electrical & wiring, machinery overhaul & repair, shafts & propellers | Joinery, furnishings, interior finishing, electronics, TV, Satcom, sourcing/ supply of fittings | Bottom cleaning & painting, deck refinishing, woodwork, sanding & varnishing | Afloat in dry dock in covered dry dock ashore under cover |

## CONSOLIDATED YACHT CORPORATION

2051 NW 11th Street
Miami, Florida 33125
USA
Tel:+1 305 643 0334
Fax:+1 305 643 1897
Email: consolidatedyacht.com

### YARD FACILITIES

| Type | Max Length | Max beam | Max weight | Max draught |
|---|---|---|---|---|
| Syncrolift | 43m (140ft) | | 400t | 4m (12ft) |
| Mobile lift | 18m (60ft) | | 35t | 2m (8ft) |
| Crane | | | 80t | |
| Serviced quay space | 46m (150ft) | | | 4m (12ft) |

### SERVICES OFFERED

| Hull & structural work in: | Engineering | Fitting-out work | Exterior work | Exterior painting |
|---|---|---|---|---|
| Aluminium, wood, composite plastics | Electrical & wiring, machinery overhaul & repair, shafts & propellers | Joinery, furnishings, interior finishing, electronics, TV, satcom, sourcing/supply of fittings | Bottom cleaning & painting, deck refinishing, woodwork, sanding & varnishing | Afloat in dry dock in covered dry dock ashore under cover |

## CONSTRUCTIONS MÉCANIQUES DE NORMANDIE (CMN)

51 Rue de la Bretonnière
BP 539
50105 Cherbourg Cedex
France
Tel:+33 2 33 88 3000
Fax:+33 2 33 88 3198
Email: tregnault@cmn-cherbourg.com

### YARD FACILITIES

| Type | Max length | Max beam | Max weight | Max draught |
|---|---|---|---|---|
| Syncrolift | 90m (295ft) | 32m (105ft) | 3,000t | 4.5m (14ft 9in) |
| Slipway | 110m (360ft) | | 1,250t | 3.6m (11ft) |
| Crane | | | 20t | |
| Serviced quay space | 320m (1,050ft) | | | 4m (13ft) |

### SERVICES OFFERED

| Hull & structural work in: | Engineering | Fitting-out work | Exterior work | Exterior painting |
|---|---|---|---|---|
| Steel, aluminium, wood, composite plastics | Pipework, tanks, electrical & wiring, machinery overhaul & repair, shafts & propellers | Joinery, furnishings, interior finishing, electronics, TV, Satcom, sourcing/ supply of fittings | Bottom cleaning & painting, deck refinishing, woodwork, sanding & varnishing | Ashore under cover |

## CRESCENT CUSTOM YACHTS

11580 Mitchell Road
Richmond
British Columbia
Canada, V6V 1T7
Tel:+1 604 324 1333
Fax:+1 604 323 7428s
Email: bcharles@arrow.cq

### YARD FACILITIES

| Type | Max Length | Max beam | Max weight | Max draught |
|---|---|---|---|---|
| Mobile lift | 46m (150ft) | | 220t | 6m (20ft) |
| Crane | | | 82t | |

### SERVICES OFFERED

| Hull & structural work in: | Engineering | Fitting-out work | Exterior work | Exterior painting |
|---|---|---|---|---|
| Composite plastics | Pipework, tanks, electrical & wiring, machinery overhaul & repair, shafts & propellers | Joinery, furnishings, interior finishing, electronics, TV, Satcom, sourcing/supply of fittings | Bottom cleaning & painting, deck refinishing, woodwork, sanding & varnishing | Ashore under cover |

## DAHM INTERNATIONAL SA

Edificio OTP
1 Muelle Viejo
E-07012 Palma de Mallorca
Baleares
Spain
Tel:+34 971 725246
Fax:+34 971 725247
Email: service@dahm-international.com

### YARD FACILITIES

| Type | Max length | Max beam | Max weight | Max draught |
|---|---|---|---|---|
| Mobile lift | 40m (131ft) | | 150t | 6m (20ft) |

### SERVICES OFFERED

| Hull & structural work in: | Engineering | Fitting-out work | Exterior work | Exterior painting |
|---|---|---|---|---|
| Steel, aluminium, wood, composite plastics | Pipework, tanks, electrical & wiring, machinery overhaul & repair, shafts & propellers, hydraulics | Joinery, furnishings, interior finishing, electronics, TV, Satcom, sourcing/ supply of fittings | Bottom cleaning & painting, deck refinishing, woodwork, sanding & varnishing | Afloat ashore under cover |

## DE GIER & BEZAAN JACHTBOUW BV

Volmolen 4
NL-1601 ET Enkhuizen
The Netherlands
Tel:+31 228 322 603
Fax:+31 228 320 462
Email: info@de-gier.nl

**YARD FACILITIES**

| Type | Max length | Max beam | Max weight | Max draught |
|---|---|---|---|---|
| Mobile lift | 25m (82ft ) | | 50t | 3.5m (11ft) |
| Crane | | | 50t | |
| Serviced quay space | 40m (131ft) | | | 3.5m (11ft) |

**SERVICES OFFERED**

| Hull & structural work in: | Engineering | Fitting-out work | Exterior work | Exterior painting |
|---|---|---|---|---|
| Steel, aluminium, wood | Pipework, tanks, electrical & wiring, machinery overhaul & repair, shafts & propellers | Joinery, furnishings, interior finishing, electronics, TV, Satcom, sourcing/ supply of fittings | Bottom cleaning & painting, deck refinishing, woodwork, sanding & varnishing | Ashore under cover |

## DELTA MARINE

1608 South 96th Street
Seattle
WA 98108
USA
Tel:+1 206 763 2383
Fax:+1 206 762 2627
Email: info@deltamarine.com

**YARD FACILITIES**

| Type | Max length | Max beam | Max weight | Max draught |
|---|---|---|---|---|
| Mobile lift | 4.8m (16ft ) | | 30t | |
| Crane | | | 100t | |
| Serviced quay space | | | | |

**SERVICES OFFERED**

| Hull & structural work in: | Engineering | Fitting-out work | Exterior work | Exterior painting |
|---|---|---|---|---|
| Steel, aluminium composite plastics | Pipework, tanks, electrical & wiring, machinery overhaul & repair, shafts & propellers | Joinery, furnishings, interior finishing, electronics, TV, Satcom, sourcing/ supply of fittings | Bottom cleaning & painting, deck refinishing, woodwork, sanding & varnishing | Ashore under cover |

## DERECKTOR OF FLORIDA

775 Taylor Lane
Dania
Florida FL 33004
USA
Tel:+1 954 920 5756
Fax:+1 954 925 1146
Email: Florida@derecktor.com

**YARD FACILITIES**

| Type | Max length | Max beam | Max weight | Max draught |
|---|---|---|---|---|
| Syncrolift | 50m (165ft) | | 600t | 3m (10ft) |
| Mobile lifts (2) | 33.5m (110ft) | | 160t & 60t | 4.6m (15ft) |
| Cranes (2) | | | 35t & 18t | |
| Serviced quay space | 46m (150ft) | | | 4.6m (15ft) |

**SERVICES OFFERED**

| Hull & structural work in: | Engineering | Fitting-out work | Exterior work | Exterior painting |
|---|---|---|---|---|
| Steel, aluminium, wood, composite plastics | Pipework, tanks, electrical & wiring, machinery overhaul & repair, shafts & propellers | Joinery, furnishings, interior finishing, electronics, TV, Satcom, sourcing/ supply of fittings | Bottom cleaning & painting, deck refinishing, woodwork, sanding & varnishing | Afloat ashore under cover |

## DERECKTOR SHIPYARDS

311 East Boston Post Road
Mamaroneck
NY 10543
USA
Tel:+1 914 698 5020
Fax:+1 914 698 4161
Email: General@derecktor.com

**YARD FACILITIES**

| Type | Max length | Max beam | Max weight | Max draught |
|---|---|---|---|---|
| Crane | | | 120t | |
| Serviced quay space | 46m (150ft) | | | 3.6m (12ft) |

**SERVICES OFFERED**

| Hull & structural work in: | Engineering | Fitting-out work | Exterior work | Exterior painting |
|---|---|---|---|---|
| Steel, aluminium, wood, composite plastics | Pipework, tanks, electrical & wiring, machinery overhaul & repair, shafts & propellers | Joinery, furnishings, interior finishing, electronics, TV, Satcom, sourcing/ supply of fittings | Bottom cleaning & painting, deck refinishing, woodwork, sanding & varnishing | Ashore under cover |

## DEVONPORT YACHTS

Devonport Royal Dockyard
Plymouth PL1 4SG
UK
Tel:+44 (0)1752 553311
Fax:+44 (0)1752 554883

### YARD FACILITIES

| Type | Max length | Max beam | Max weight | Max draught |
|---|---|---|---|---|
| Dry docks (14) | 215m (705ft) | 28m (92ft) | | 11m (36ft) |
| Mobile lift | 24m (79ft) | | 50t | |
| Cranes | | | 150t | |
| Serviced quay space | 230m (755ft) | | | 11m (36ft) |

### SERVICES OFFERED

| Hull & structural work in: | Engineering | Fitting-out work | Exterior work | Exterior painting |
|---|---|---|---|---|
| Steel, aluminium, wood, composite plastics | Pipework, tanks, electrical & wiring, machinery overhaul & repair, shafts & propellers | Joinery, furnishings, interior finishing, electronics, TV, Satcom, sourcing/ supply of fittings | Bottom cleaning & painting, deck refinishing, woodwork, sanding & varnishing | Afloat in dry dock in covered dry dock ashore under cover |

## ERMAR MALLORCA SL

Muelle Viejo
Espigon Exterior
E-07012
Palma de Mallorca
Spain
Tel:+34 971 72 82 84
Fax:+34 971 72 19 96
Email: schwizer@schwizer.com

### YARD FACILITIES

| Type | Max Length | Max beam | Max weight | Max draught |
|---|---|---|---|---|
| Dry dock | | | | |
| Mobile lift | | | | |

### SERVICES OFFERED

| Hull & structural work in: | Engineering | Fitting-out work | Exterior work | Exterior painting |
|---|---|---|---|---|
| Steel, aluminium, wood, composite plastics | | | Bottom cleaning & painting, woodwork, sanding & varnishing | |

## FAIRLIE RESTORATIONS LTD

Unit 17
Port Hamble
Hamble
Hampshire SO31 4NN
UK
Tel:+44 (0)23 80456336
Fax:+44 (0)23 80456166
Email: info@fairlierestore.demon.co.uk

### YARD FACILITIES

| Type | Max length | Max leam | Max weight | Max draught |
|---|---|---|---|---|
| Mobile lift | 33m (108ft) | | 60t | |
| Serviced quay space | 35m (115ft) | | | 5m (16ft) |

### SERVICES OFFERED

| Hull & structural work in: | Engineering | Fitting-out work | Exterior work | Exterior painting |
|---|---|---|---|---|
| Steel, wood | Pipework, tanks, electrical & wiring, machinery overhaul & repair, shafts & propellers | Joinery, furnishing interior finishing, electronics, TV, Satcom, sourcing/ supply of fittings | Bottom cleaning & painting, deck refinishing, woodwork, sanding & varnishing | Afloat ashore under cover |

## FEADSHIP

PO Box 70
2110 AB Aerdenhout
The Netherlands
Tel:+31 23 5247000
Fax:+31 23 5248639
Email: info@feadship.nl

### YARD FACILITIES

| Type | Max length | Max beam | Max weight | Max draught |
|---|---|---|---|---|
| Dry docks (3) | 100m (328ft) | 14m (46ft) | | 3.4m (11ft) |
| Slipways (3) | 65m (213ft) | | 800t | 3.4m (11ft) |
| Cranes (12) | | | 10t | |
| Serviced quay space | 150m (492ft) | | | 4.5m (15ft) |

### SERVICES OFFERED

| Hull & structural work in: | Engineering | Fitting-out work | Exterior work | Exterior painting |
|---|---|---|---|---|
| Steel, aluminium, wood | Pipework, tanks, electrical & wiring, machinery overhaul & repair, shafts & propellers | Joinery, furnishings, interior finishing, electronics, TV, Satcom, sourcing/ supply of fittings | Bottom cleaning & painting, deck refinishing, woodwork, sanding & varnishing | In covered dry dock |

## FOSELEV MARINE

ZIP de Bregaillon
83500 La Seyne Sur Mer
France
Tel:+33 494 11 50 50
Fax:+33 494 30 13 83
Email: info@foselevmarine.com

### YARD FACILITIES

| Type | Max Length | Max beam | Max weight | Max draught |
|---|---|---|---|---|
| Dry dock | 75m (246ft) | 15.50m (51ft) | | 4.50m (15ft) |
| Cranes (2) | | | 12t | |
| Serviced quay space | 210m (689ft) | | | 5.5m (18ft) |

### SERVICES OFFERED

| Hull & structural work in: | Engineering | Fitting-out work | Exterior work | Exterior painting |
|---|---|---|---|---|
| Steel, aluminium, wood | Pipework, tanks, electrical & wiring, machinery overhaul & repair, shafts & propellers | | Bottom cleaning & painting, deck refinishing | Afloat<br>in dry dock<br>in covered dry dock |

## GRANDWELD

PO Box 24755
Dubai
United Arab Emirates
Tel:+971 4 324 1707
Fax:+971 4 324 1706
Email: atos@emirates.net.ae

### YARD FACILITIES

| Type | Max Length | Max beam | Max weight | Max draught |
|---|---|---|---|---|
| Syncrolift | 110m (361ft) | | 2,530t | 5m (16ft) |
| Crane | | | 400t | |
| Serviced quay space | 600m (1,969ft) | | | 5m (16ft) |

### SERVICES OFFERED

| Hull & structural work in: | Engineering | Fitting-out work | Exterior work | Exterior painting |
|---|---|---|---|---|
| Steel, aluminium, wood, composite plastics | Pipework, tanks electrical & wiring, machinery overhaul & repair, shafts & propellers | Joinery, furnishings, interior finishing, electronics, TV, Satcom, supply of fittings | Bottom cleaning & painting, deck refinishing, woodwork, sanding & varnishing | Afloat<br>in dry dock<br>in covered dry dock<br>ashore under cover |

## HAKVOORT SHIPYARD

Havenstraat 17-22
1141 AX Monnickendam
The Netherlands
Tel:+31 299 651403
Fax:+31 299 651041
Email: Hakvoort@compuserve.com

### YARD FACILITIES

| Type | Max length | Max beam | Max weight | Max draught |
|---|---|---|---|---|
| Slipway | 50m (164ft) | | 400t | 3m (10ft) |
| Crane | | | 20t | |
| Serviced quay space | 60m (197ft) | | | 3m (10ft) |

### SERVICES OFFERED

| Hull & structural work in: | Engineering | Fitting-out work | Exterior work | Exterior painting |
|---|---|---|---|---|
| Steel, aluminium | Pipework, tanks, electrical & wiring, machinery overhaul & repair, shafts & propellers | Joinery, furnishings, interior finishing, electronics, TV, Satcom, sourcing/ supply of fittings | Bottom cleaning & painting, deck refinishing, woodwork, sanding & varnishing | In covered dry dock |

## HELI YACHTS

SV Polikarpa 8
52100 Pula
Croatia
Tel:+385 52 216633
Fax:+385 52 216634
Email: info@heliyachts.com

### YARD FACILITIES

| Type | Max length | Max beam | Max weight | Max draught |
|---|---|---|---|---|
| Mobile lift | | | 220t | |
| Crane | | | 120t | |
| Serviced quay space | 200m (656ft) | | | 7m (23ft) |

### SERVICES OFFERED

| Hull & structural work in: | Engineering | Fitting-out work | Exterior work | Exterior painting |
|---|---|---|---|---|
| Steel, aluminium, wood | Pipework, tanks, electrical & wiring, machinery overhaul & repair, shafts & propellers | Joinery, furnishings, interior finishing, electronics, TV, Satcom, sourcing/ supply of fittings | Bottom cleaning & painting, deck refinishing, woodwork, sanding & varnishing | Afloat<br>ashore under cover<br>paint shed |

## THE HINCKLEY CO

Service Department
PO Box 699
130 Shore Road
Southwest Harbor
ME 04679, USA
Tel:+1 207 244 5572
Fax:+1 207 244 9433
Email: service@thehinckleyco.com

### YARD FACILITIES

| Type | Max Length | Max beam | Max weight | Max draught |
|---|---|---|---|---|
| Mobile lift (3) | 40m (130ft) | 9.75m (32ft) | 160t | 3.6m (12ft) |
| Crane | | | 20t | |

### SERVICES OFFERED

| Hull & structural work in: | Engineering | Fitting-out work | Exterior work | Exterior painting |
|---|---|---|---|---|
| Steel, aluminium, wood, composite plastics | Pipework, tanks, electrical & wiring, machinery overhaul & repair, shafts & propellers | Joinery, furnishings, interior finishing, electronics, TV, Satcom, sourcing/ supply of fittings | Bottom cleaning & painting, deck refinishing, woodwork, sanding & varnishing | Ashore under cover |

## INTERMARINE SAVANNAH

301 North Lathrop Avenue
Savannah, GA 31415, USA
Tel:+1 912 234 6579
Fax:+1 912 236 8887
Email: imsav_conboy@compuserve.com

### YARD FACILITIES

| Type | Max length | Max beam | Max weight | Max draught |
|---|---|---|---|---|
| Dry dock | 155m (500ft) | 20m (65ft) | | 7.5m (25ft) |
| Syncrolift | 61m (200ft) | | 1,100t | 7m (23ft) |
| Crane | | | 100t | |
| Serviced quay space | 155m (130ft) | | | 12m (40ft) |

### SERVICES OFFERED

| Hull & structural work in: | Engineering | Fitting-out work | Exterior work | Exterior painting |
|---|---|---|---|---|
| Steel, aluminium, wood, composite plastics | Pipework, tanks, electrical & wiring, machinery overhaul & repair, shafts & propellers | Joinery, furnishings, interior finishing, electronics, TV, Satcom, sourcing/ supply of fittings | Bottom cleaning & painting, deck refinishing, woodwork, sanding & varnishing | Afloat in dry dock ashore under cover |

## INTERNATIONAL MARINE SERVICES (IMS)

Le Pin Rolland
83430 Saint Mandrier
France
Tel:+33 494 30 54 94
Fax:+33 494 30 52 08
Email: info@ims.fr

### YARD FACILITIES

| Type | Max length | Max beam | Max weight | Max draught |
|---|---|---|---|---|
| Mobile lift | 50m (164ft) | | 320t | 4m (13ft) |
| Crane | | | 8t | |
| Serviced quay space | 200m (656ft) | | | 4m (13ft) |

### SERVICES OFFERED

| Hull & structural work in: | Engineering | Fitting-out work | Exterior work | Exterior painting |
|---|---|---|---|---|
| Steel, aluminium, wood | Pipework, tanks, electrical & wiring, machinery overhaul & repair, shafts & propellers | Joinery, furnishings, interior finishing, electronics, TV, Satcom, sourcing/ supply of fittings | Bottom cleaning & painting, deck refinishing, woodwork, sanding & varnishing | Afloat ashore under cover |

## IZAR

San Fernando Shipyard
Ctra de la Carraca s/n
11100 San Fernando – Cadiz
Spain
Tel:+34 956 599 897
Fax:+34 956 599 898
Email: comercialsf@izar.es

### YARD FACILITIES

| Type | Max length | Max beam | Max weight | Max draught |
|---|---|---|---|---|
| Dry dock | 147m (482ft) | 23.9m (78ft) | | |
| Slipway | 156m (512ft) | | | |
| Crane | | | 100t | |
| Serviced quay | 775m (2,543ft) | | | 7m (23ft) |

### SERVICES OFFERED

| Hull & structural work in: | Engineering | Fitting-out work | Exterior work | Exterior painting |
|---|---|---|---|---|
| Steel, aluminium, wood composite plastics | Pipework, tanks, electrical & wiring, machinery overhaul & repair, shafts & propellers | Joinery, furnishings, interior finishing, electronics, TV, Satcom, sourcing/ supply of fittings | Bottom cleaning & painting, deck refinishing, woodwork & varnishing | Afloat in covered dry dock ashore under cover |

## JFA

Quai du Moros
Rive Gauche
29900 Concarneau
France
Tel:+33 2 98 60 49 48
Fax:+33 2 98 60 49 40
Email: jfa.cn@wanadoo.fr

### YARD FACILITIES

| Type | Max length | Max beam | Max weight | Max draught |
|---|---|---|---|---|
| Syncrolift | 100m (328ft) | 13m (43ft) | 2,000t | 7m (23ft) |
| Slipway | 40m (130ft) | | 400t | 4.5m (15ft) |
| Crane | | | 200t | |
| Serviced quay space | 100m (328ft) | | | 6m (20ft) |

### SERVICES OFFERED

| Hull & structural work in: | Engineering | Fitting-out work | Exterior work | Exterior painting |
|---|---|---|---|---|
| Steel, aluminium, wood, composite plastics | Pipework, tanks, electrical & wiring, machinery overhaul & repair, shafts & propellers | Joinery, furnishings, interior finishing, electronics, TV, Satcom, sourcing/ supply of fittings | Bottom cleaning & painting, deck refinishing, woodwork, sanding & varnishing | Ashore under cover |

## JONES BOAT YARD INC

3399 NW South River Drive
Miami, Florida 33142
USA
Tel:+1 305 635 0891
Fax:+1 305 633 6758
Email: mail@jonesdrydock.com

### YARD FACILITIES

| Type | Max Length | Max beam | Max weight | Max draught |
|---|---|---|---|---|
| Dry dock (2) | 78m (256ft) | 16.46m (54ft) | | 3.65m (12ft) |
| Syncrolift | 30.48m (100ft) | | 150t | 2.44m (8ft) |
| Mobile lift | 19.81m (65ft) | | 60t | 2.13m (7ft) |
| Crane | | | | |

### SERVICES OFFERED

| Hull & structural work in: | Engineering | Fitting-out work | Exterior work | Exterior painting |
|---|---|---|---|---|
| Steel, aluminium, wood, composite plastics | Pipework, tanks, electrical & wiring, shafts & propellers | Sourcing/supply of fittings | Bottom cleaning & painting, deck refinishing, woodwork sanding & varnishing | Afloat in dry dock |

## D N KELLEY & SON INC SHIPYARD

32 Water Street, Fairhaven
MA 02719
USA
Tel:+1 508 999 6266
Fax:+1 508 999 2513
Email: dnkhaul@AOL.com

### YARD FACILITIES

| Type | Max length | Max beam | Max weight | Max draught |
|---|---|---|---|---|
| Slipway | 61m (200ft) | 14m (46ft) | 800t | 5.5m (18ft) |
| Mobile lift | 33.5m (110ft) | 7.9m (26ft) | 160t | 3m (10ft) |
| Serviced quay space | 244m (800ft) | | | 5.5m (18ft) |

### SERVICES OFFERED

| Hull & structural work in: | Engineering | Fitting-out work | Exterior work | Exterior painting |
|---|---|---|---|---|
| Steel, aluminium, wood, composite plastics | Pipework, tanks, electrical & wiring, machinery overhaul & repair, shafts & propellers | Joinery, sourcing/supply of fittings | Bottom cleaning & painting, deck refinishing, woodwork, sanding & varnishing | Afloat in dry dock ashore under cover |

## LITTLE HARBOR MARINE

1 Little Harbor Landing
Portsmouth, RI, USA
Tel:+1 401 683 7100
Fax:+1 401 683 7118
Email: inquiries@thco.com

### YARD FACILITIES

| Type | Max length | Max beam | Max weight | Max draught |
|---|---|---|---|---|
| Mobile lift | 42.6m (140ft) | | 160t | 5.2m (17ft) |
| Crane | | | 18t | |
| Serviced quay space | 150m (492ft) | | | 9m (30ft) |

### SERVICES OFFERED

| Hull & structural work in: | Engineering | Fitting-out work | Exterior work | Exterior painting |
|---|---|---|---|---|
| Steel, aluminium, wood, composite plastics | Pipework, tanks, electrical & wiring, machinery overhaul & repair, shafts & propellers | Joinery, furnishings, interior finishing, electronics, TV, Satcom, sourcing/ supply of fittings | Bottom cleaning & painting, deck refinishing, woodwork, sanding & varnishing | Afloat ashore under cover |

## LÜRSSEN WERFT

Fr Klippertstrasse 1
28759 Bremen
Germany
Tel:+49 421 6604 166
Fax:+49 421 6604 170
Email: UY@lurssen.de

### YARD FACILITIES

| Type | Max length | Max beam | Max weight | Max draught |
|---|---|---|---|---|
| Dry dock (covered) | 170m (558ft) | 25m (82ft) | | 8m (26ft) |
| Syncrolift | 100m (328ft) | | 1,800t | 7m (23ft) |
| Crane | | | - | |
| Serviced quay space | unlimited | | | 10m (33ft) |

### SERVICES OFFERED

| Hull & structural work in: | Engineering | Fitting-out work | Exterior work | Exterior painting |
|---|---|---|---|---|
| Steel, aluminium, wood, composite plastics | Pipework, tanks, electrical & wiring, machinery overhaul & repair, shafts & propellers | Joinery, furnishings, interior finishing, electronics, TV, Satcom, sourcing/ supply of fittings | Bottom cleaning & painting, deck refinishing, woodwork, sanding & varnishing | In covered dry dock ashore under cover |

## LUS-BEN-AZIMUT

Via M Coppino 441
55049 Viareggio
Italy
Tel:+39 0584 384111/2
Fax:+39 0584 396458

### YARD FACILITIES

| Type | Max length | Max beam | Max weight | Max draught |
|---|---|---|---|---|
| Mobile lift | 60m (197ft) | 10.5m (34ft) | 500t | 4m (13ft) |
| Crane | | | 20t | |
| Serviced quay space | 50m (164ft) | | 4m (13ft) | |

### SERVICES OFFERED

| Hull & structural work in: | Engineering | Fitting-out work | Exterior work | Exterior painting |
|---|---|---|---|---|
| Steel, aluminium, wood, composite plastics | Pipework, tanks, electrical & wiring, machinery overhaul & repair, shafts & propellers | Joinery, furnishings, interior finishing, electronics, TV, Satcom, sourcing/ supply of fittings | Bottom cleaning & painting, deck refinishing, woodwork, sanding & varnishing | Afloat ashore under cover |

## MCMULLEN & WING LTD

21 Gabador Place
Mt Wellington
Auckland 6
New Zealand
Tel:+64 9 573 1405
Fax:+64 9 573 0393
Email: mcwing.boats@xtra.co.nz

### YARD FACILITIES

| Type | Max length | Max beam | Max weight | Max draught |
|---|---|---|---|---|
| Slipway | 45m (150ft) | | 300t | 3.8m (12ft) |
| Mobile lift | 30m (100ft) | | 70t | 4.3m (14ft) |
| Serviced quay space | 45m (150ft) | | | 4.3m (14ft) |

### SERVICES OFFERED

| Hull & structural work in: | Engineering | Fitting-out work | Exterior work | Exterior painting |
|---|---|---|---|---|
| Steel, aluminium, composite plastics | Pipework, tanks, electrical & wiring, machinery overhaul & repair, shafts & propellers | Joinery, furnishings, interior finishing, sourcing/ supply of fittings | Bottom cleaning & painting, deck refinishing, woodwork, sanding & varnishing | Ashore under cover |

## MANOEL ISLAND YACHT YARD

Manoel Island
Gzira
Malta GZR03
Tel:+356 334 453 / 332828
Fax:+356 343 900
Email: info@yachtyard-malta.com

### YARD FACILITIES

| Type | Max length | Max beam | Max weight | Max draught |
|---|---|---|---|---|
| Dry dock | 262m (860ft) | 40m (131ft) | | 8.5m (28ft) |
| Slipway | 55m (180ft) | | 450t | 4m (13ft) |
| Mobile lift | 17m (56ft) | | 45t | 2.7m (9ft) |
| Crane | | | 12t | |
| Serviced quay space | 66m (216ft) | | | 6m (20ft) |

### SERVICES OFFERED

| Hull & structural work in: | Engineering | Fitting-out work | Exterior work | Exterior painting |
|---|---|---|---|---|
| Steel, aluminium, wood, composite plastics | Pipework, tanks, electrical & wiring, machinery overhaul & repair, shafts & propellers | Joinery, furnishings, interior finishing, electronics, TV, Satcom, sourcing/ supply of fittings | Bottom cleaning & painting, deck refinishing, woodwork, sanding & varnishing | Afloat in dry dock ashore under cover |

## MARINA BARCELONA

PO Juan de Borbon No92
08003 Barcelona
Spain
Tel:+34 932 214370
Fax:+34 932 215650
Email: MB92@bcn.servicom.es

### YARD FACILITIES

| Type | Max length | Max beam | Max weight | Max draught |
|---|---|---|---|---|
| Dry dock | 200m (761ft) | 30m (114ft) | | 8m (30ft) |
| Syncrolift | 80m (305ft) | 14.5m (48ft) | 2,000t | 6m (23ft) |
| Mobile lift | 40m (152ft) | 7.7m (25ft) | 150t | 4m (15ft) |
| Crane | | | 12t | |
| Serviced quay space | 120m (457ft) | | | 12m (46ft) |

### SERVICES OFFERED

| Hull & structural work in: | Engineering | Fitting-out work | Exterior work | Exterior painting |
|---|---|---|---|---|
| Steel, aluminium, wood, composite plastics | Pipework, tanks, electrical & wiring, machinery overhaul & repair, shafts & propellers | Joinery, furnishings, interior finishing, electronics, TV, Satcom, sourcing/ supply of fittings | Bottom cleaning & painting, deck refinishing, woodwork, sanding & varnishing | Ashore & afloat under cover. (All painting work carried out by Pinmar SA) |

## MARSIC SHIPYARD (MONDO GROUP)

Via L Cibrario
16154 Genova
Italy
Tel:+39 010 650660
Fax:+39 010 6512651
Email: massimo@marsic.it

### YARD FACILITIES

| Type | Max length | Max beam | Max weight | Max draught |
|---|---|---|---|---|
| Slipway | 40m (131ft) | | 350t | 4.20m (14ft) |
| Crane (2) | | | 15t | |
| Serviced quay space | 55m (180ft) | | | 4m (13ft) |

### SERVICES OFFERED

| Hull & structural work in: | Engineering | Fitting-out work | Exterior work | Exterior painting |
|---|---|---|---|---|
| Steel, aluminium, wood, composite plastics | Pipework, tanks, electrical & wiring, machinery overhaul & repair, shaft & propellers | Joinery, furnishings, interior finishing, electronics, TV, Satcom. sourcing/ supply of fittings | Bottom cleaning & painting, deck refinishing, woodwork, sanding & varnishing | Afloat ashore under cover |

## MERRILL-STEVENS DRY DOCK CO

1270 NW 11th St
Miami, FL 33125, USA
Tel:+1 305 324 5211
Fax:+1 305 326 8911
Email: msddmiami@aol.com

### YARD FACILITIES

| Type | Max length | Max beam | Max weight | Max draught |
|---|---|---|---|---|
| Dry dock / elevator | 49m (160ft) | 8.5m (28ft) | 500t | 4m (13ft) |
| Slipway | 49m (160ft) | 12m (40ft) | 500t | 3.6m (12ft) |
| Mobile lift | 20m (65ft) | 7m (23ft) | 70t | |
| Crane (mobile) | | | 15t | |
| Serviced quay space | 457m (1,500ft) | | | 4.3m (14ft) |

### SERVICES OFFERED

| Hull & structural work in: | Engineering | Fitting-out work | Exterior work | Exterior painting |
|---|---|---|---|---|
| Steel, aluminium, wood, composite plastics | Pipework, tanks, electrical & wiring, machinery overhaul & repair, shafts & propellers | Joinery, furnishings, interior finishing, electronics, TV, Satcom, sourcing/ supply of fittings | Bottom cleaning & painting, deck refinishing, woodwork, sanding & varnishing | Afloat in covered dry dock ashore under cover |

## MONACO MARINE FRANCE – RIVIERA YACHT SERVICES

Port de Plaisance
Beaulieu sur Mer
France
Tel:+33 493 764764
Fax:+33 493 764765
Email: RYS@monaco-marine.com

### YARD FACILITIES

| Type | Max Length | Max beam | Max weight | Max draught |
|---|---|---|---|---|
| Dry dock | 40m (131ft) | 8m (26ft) | | 3m (10ft) |
| Mobile lift | | | 100t | |
| Crane | | | 3t | |
| Serviced quay space | 60m (197ft) | | | 4.5m (15ft) |

### SERVICES OFFERED

| Hull & structural work in: | Engineering | Fitting-out work | Exterior work | Exterior painting |
|---|---|---|---|---|
| Steel, aluminium, wood, composite plastics | Pipework, tanks, electrical & wiring, machinery overhaul & repair, shafts & propellers | Joinery, furnishings, interior finishing, sourcing/supply of fittings | Bottom cleaning & painting, deck refinishing, woodwork, sanding & varninshing | Afloat in dry dock in covered dry dock ashore under cover |

## NEW ZEALAND YACHTS LTD

279 Port Road, Whangarei
New Zealand
Tel:+64 9 430 3148
Fax:+64 9 4303147
Email: info@newzealandyachts.com

### YARD FACILITIES

| Type | Max length | Max beam | Max weight | Max draught |
|---|---|---|---|---|
| Slipway | 80m (262ft) | | 2,000t | 4.0m (13ft) |
| Crane | | | 300t | |

### SERVICES OFFERED

| Hull & structural work in: | Engineering | Fitting-out work | Exterior work | Exterior painting |
|---|---|---|---|---|
| Steel, aluminium, wood, composite plastics | Pipework, tanks, electrical & wiring, machinery overhaul & repair, shaft & propellers | Joinery, furnishings, interior finishing, electronics, TV, Satcom, sourcing/ supply of fittings | Bottom cleaning & painting, deck refinishing, woodwork sanding & varnishing | Afloat in dry dock in covered dry dock |

## NOAKES BOAT & SHIPYARD

PO Box 1644
North Sydney
NSW 2059
Australia
Tel:+61 2 9925 0306
Fax:+61 2 9929 6028
Email: noakesboat@bigpond.com

### YARD FACILITIES

| Type | Max length | Max beam | Max weight | Max draught |
|---|---|---|---|---|
| Slipway | 40m (131ft) | 10m (30ft) | 155t | 6m (20ft) |
| Mobile lift | 30m (98ft) | 6.7m (22ft) | 80t | 8m (16ft) |
| Crane | | | 18t | |
| Serviced quay space | 30m (98ft) | | | 5m (16ft) |

### SERVICES OFFERED

| Hull & structural work in: | Engineering | Fitting-out work | Exterior work | Exterior painting |
|---|---|---|---|---|
| Steel, aluminium, wood, composite plastics | Pipework, tanks, electrical & wiring, machinery overhaul & repair, shafts & propellers | Joinery, furnishings, interior finishing, electronics, TV, Satcom, sourcing/ supply of fittings | Bottom cleaning & painting, deck refinishing, woodwork, sanding & varnishing | Afloat ashore under cover |

## NORTHPORT ENGINEERING

PO Box 848
Whangarei
New Zealand
Tel:+64 9 438 1279
Fax:+64 9 438 7067
Email: johnhutchinson@northlandportcorp.co.nz

### YARD FACILITIES

| Type | Max length | Max beam | Max weight | Max draught |
|---|---|---|---|---|
| Slipways (3) | 76m (249ft) | | 1,800t | 6m (20ft) |
| Crane | | | 40/50t | |
| Serviced quay space | 160m (525ft) | | | 12m (39ft) |

### SERVICES OFFERED

| Hull & structural work in: | Engineering | Fitting-out work | Exterior work | Exterior painting |
|---|---|---|---|---|
| Steel, aluminium | Pipework, tanks, electrical & wiring, machinery overhaul & repair, shafts & propellers | Joinery, furnishings, interior finishing, electronics, TV, Satcom, sourcing/ supply of fittings | Bottom cleaning & painting, deck refinishing, woodwork, sanding & varnishing | Afloat ashore under cover |

## PALMER JOHNSON SAVANNAH

3124 River Drive
Savannah
GA 31404
USA
Tel:+1 912 352 4956
Fax:+1 912 354 8621
Email: skip@pjsavannah.com

### YARD FACILITIES

| Type | Max length | Max beam | Max weight | Max draught |
|---|---|---|---|---|
| Syncrolift | 58m (190ft) | | 1,150t | 5m (16ft) |
| Mobile lift | 36.5m (120ft) | | 160t | 5m (16ft) |
| Crane | | | 100t | |
| Serviced quay space | 100m (328ft) | | 5m (16ft) | |

### SERVICES OFFERED

| Hull & structural work in: | Engineering | Fitting-out work | Exterior work | Exterior painting |
|---|---|---|---|---|
| Steel, aluminium, wood | Pipework, tanks, electrical & wiring, machinery overhaul & repair, shafts & propellers | Joinery, furnishings, interior finishing, electronics, TV, Satcom, sourcing/ supply of fittings | Bottom cleaning & painting, deck refinishing, woodwork, sanding & varnishing | Ashore under cover |

## PENDENNIS SHIPYARD

The Docks
Falmouth
Cornwall TR11 4NB
UK
Tel:+44 (0)1326 211344
Fax:+44 (0)1326 319253
Email: info@pendennis.com

### YARD FACILITIES

| Type | Max length | Max beam | Max weight | Max draught |
|---|---|---|---|---|
| Slipway | 65m (213ft) | 10m (33ft) | 500t | 5m (16ft) |
| Mobile lift | 24.5m (80ft) | 6m (20ft) | 60t | 3m (10ft) |
| Crane | | | 48t | |
| Serviced quay space | 85m (279ft), open | 17m (56ft) | | 4.5m (15ft) |
| | 70m (230ft), covered | | | |

### SERVICES OFFERED

| Hull & structural work in: | Engineering | Fitting-out work | Exterior work | Exterior painting |
|---|---|---|---|---|
| Steel, aluminium, wood, composite plastics | Pipework, tanks, electrical & wiring, machinery overhaul & repair, shafts & propellers | Joinery, furnishings, interior finishing, electronics, TV, Satcom, sourcing/ supply of equipment | Bottom cleaning & painting, deck refinishing, woodwork, sanding & varnishing | Afloat in covered dry dock ashore under cover |

## PENGUIN BOAT INTERNATIONAL

11 Tuas Crescent
Singapore
638705
Tel:+65 8680 629
Fax:+65 863 3438

### YARD FACILITIES

| Type | Max length | Max beam | Max weight | Max draught |
|---|---|---|---|---|
| Mobile lift | 55m (180ft) | 15.8m (51ft 10in) | 500t | 3m (10ft) |
| Serviced quay space | 40m (131ft) | 48m (157ft) | | 3m (10ft) |

### SERVICES OFFERED

| Hull & structural work in: | Engineering | Fitting-out work | Exterior work | Exterior painting |
|---|---|---|---|---|
| Aluminium, wood, composite plastics | Pipework, tanks, electrical & wiring, shafts & propellers | | Bottom cleaning & painting | Afloat ashore under cover |

## PENZANCE DRY DOCK

Wharf Road
Penzance
Cornwall TR18 4BW
UK
Tel:+44 (0)1736 363838
Fax:+44 (0)1736 351207

### YARD FACILITIES

| Type | Max length | Max beam | Max weight | Max draught |
|---|---|---|---|---|
| Dry dock | 74m (243ft) | 11m (36ft) | | 3.7m (12ft) |
| Crane | | | 8/25t | |
| Serviced quay space | 120m (394ft) | | | 5.5m (18ft) |

### SERVICES OFFERED

| Hull & structural work in: | Engineering | Fitting-out work | Exterior work | Exterior painting |
|---|---|---|---|---|
| Steel, aluminium, wood | Pipework, tanks, electrical & wiring, machinery overhaul & repair, shafts & propellers | Joinery, furnishings, interior finishing, electronics, TV, Satcom, sourcing/ supply of fittings | Bottom cleaning & painting, deck refinishing, woodwork, sanding & varnishing | Afloat in dry dock |

## PERINI NAVI

Via Coppino 114
55049 Viareggio
Italy
Tel:+39 0584 4241
Fax:+39 0584 424200
Email: sales@perininavi.it

### YARD FACILITIES

| Type | Max length | Max beam | Max weight | Max draught |
|---|---|---|---|---|
| Syncrolift | 65m (213ft) | 13.5m (44ft) | 700t | 4.5m (15ft) |
| Serviced quay space | 70m (230ft) | | | 4.5m (15ft) |

### SERVICES OFFERED

| Hull & structural work in: | Engineering | Fitting-out work | Exterior work | Exterior painting |
|---|---|---|---|---|
| Steel, aluminium, wood | Pipework, tanks, electrical & wiring, machinery overhaul & repair, shafts & propellers | Joinery, furnishings, interior finishing, electronics, TV, Satcom, sourcing/ supply of fittings | Bottom cleaning & painting, deck refinishing, woodwork, sanding & varnishing | Afloat in dry dock in covered dry dock ashore under cover |

## PLATYPUS MARINE INC

1441 N Northlake Way, Suite 220
Seattle, WA 98178, USA
Tel:+1 206 633 1073
Fax:+1 206 633 1283
Email: info@platypusmarine.com

**YARD FACILITIES**

| Type | Max length | Max beam | Max weight | Max draught |
|---|---|---|---|---|
| Mobile lift | 50m (164ft) | | 330t | |

**SERVICES OFFERED**

| Hull & structural work in: | Engineering | Fitting-out work | Exterior work | Exterior painting |
|---|---|---|---|---|
| Steel, aluminium, wood | Pipework, tanks, electrical & wiring, shafts & propellers | Joinery, furnishings, interior finishing, electronics, TV, Satcom, sourcing/ supply of fittings | Bottom cleaning & painting, deck refinishing, woodwork, sanding & varnishing | Afloat in dry dock ashore under cover |

## REFIT NEW ZEALAND LTD

1 Den Place
PO Box 14030
Tauranga
New Zealand
Tel:+64 7 577 1186
Fax:+64 7 577 1189
Email: refitnz@refitnz.co.nz

**YARD FACILITIES**

| Type | Max length | Max beam | Max weight | Max draught |
|---|---|---|---|---|
| Slipway | 60m (197ft) | | 600t | 5.8m (19ft) |
| Serviced quay space | 60m (197ft) | | | 6.0m (20ft) |

**SERVICES OFFERED**

| Hull & structural work in: | Engineering | Fitting-out work | Exterior work | Exterior painting |
|---|---|---|---|---|
| Steel, aluminium, wood, composite plastics | Pipework, tanks, electrical & wiring, machinery overhaul & repair, shafts & propellers | Joinery, furnishings, interior finishing, electronics, TV, Satcom, sourcing/ supply of fittings | Bottom cleaning & painting, deck refinishing, woodwork, sanding & varnishing | Ashore, not under cover |

## ROLLY MARINE SERVICE INC

2551 State Road 84
Fort Lauderdale
FL 33312
USA
Tel:+1 954 583 5300
Fax:+1 954 791 5094

**YARD FACILITIES**

| Type | Max length | Max beam | Max weight | Max draught |
|---|---|---|---|---|
| Mobile lift | 45m (150ft) | 8.8m (29ft) | 200t | 2.7m (9ft) |
| Crane | | | 100t | |
| Serviced quay space | 40m (130ft) | | | 2.7m (9ft) |

**SERVICES OFFERED**

| Hull & structural work in: | Engineering | Fitting-out work | Exterior work | Exterior painting |
|---|---|---|---|---|
| Steel, aluminium, composite plastics | Pipework, tanks, electrical & wiring, machinery overhaul & repair, shafts & propellers | Joinery, furnishings, interior finishing, electronics, TV, Satcom, sourcing/ supply of fittings | Bottom cleaning & painting, deck refinishing, woodwork, sanding & varnishing | Afloat in dry dock in covered dry dock ashore under cover |

## ROSCIOLI INTERNATIONAL INC

3201 SR 84
Fort Lauderdale
FL 33312
USA
Tel:+1 954 581 9200
Fax:+1 954 791 0958

**YARD FACILITIES**

| Type | Max length | Max beam | Max weight | Max draught |
|---|---|---|---|---|
| Dry dock | 35m (115ft) | 24m (79ft) | | 2.1m (7ft) |
| Slipway & mobile lift | 35m (115ft) | | 150t | 2.1m (7ft) |
| Syncrolift | 35m (115ft) | | 150t | 2.1m (7ft) |
| Crane | | | 150t | |
| Serviced quay space | 35m (115ft) | | | 2.1m (7ft) |

**SERVICES OFFERED**

| Hull & structural work in: | Engineering | Fitting-out work | Exterior work | Exterior painting |
|---|---|---|---|---|
| Steel, aluminium, wood, composite plastics | Pipework, tanks, electrical & wiring, machinery overhaul & repair, shafts & propellers | Joinery, furnishings, interior finishing, electronics, TV, Satcom, sourcing/ supply of fittings | Bottom cleaning & painting, deck refinishing, woodwork, sanding & varnishing | Afloat in dry dock in covered dry dock ashore under cover |

## ROYAL HUISMAN SHIPYARD

Flevo weg 1, P.O.Box 23
8325 ZG Vollenhove
The Netherlands
Tel:+31 527 243131
Fax:+31 527 243800
Email: yachts@royalhuisman.com

**YARD FACILITIES**

| Type | Max length | Max beam | Max weight | Max draught |
|---|---|---|---|---|
| Cranes | | | 2 x 500t | |
| Serviced quay space | 60m (197ft) | | | 4.8m (16ft) |

**SERVICES OFFERED**

| Hull & structural work in: | Engineering | Fitting-out work | Exterior work | Exterior painting |
|---|---|---|---|---|
| Aluminium, composite plastics | Pipework, tanks, electrical & wiring, machinery overhaul & repair, shafts & propellers | Joinery, furnishings, interior finishing, electronics, TV, Satcom, sourcing/ supply of fittings | Bottom cleaning & painting, deck refinishing, woodwork, sanding & varnishing | Ashore under cover |

## RYBOVICH SPENCER

4200 North Flager Drive
West Palm Beach
FL 33407
USA
Tel:+1 561 844 1800
Fax:+1 561 844 8393
Email: service@rybovich.com

**YARD FACILITIES**

| Type | Max length | Max beam | Max weight | Max draught |
|---|---|---|---|---|
| Syncrolift | 35m (115ft) | 4.7m (23ft) | 160t | 3.5m (12ft) |
| Mobile lift | 50m (164ft) | 9.2m (45ft) | 300t | 4m (13ft) |
| Serviced quay space | 65m (213ft) | | | 4m (13ft) |

**SERVICES OFFERED**

| Hull & structural work in: | Engineering | Fitting-out work | Exterior work | Exterior painting |
|---|---|---|---|---|
| Steel, aluminium, wood, composite plastics | Pipework, tanks, electrical & wiring, machinery overhaul & repair, shafts & propellers | Joinery, furnishings, interior finishing, electronics, TV, Satcom, sourcing/ supply of fittings | Bottom cleaning & painting, deck refinishing, woodwork, sanding & varnishing | Ashore in dry dock in covered dry dock ashore under cover |

## ST AUGUSTINE MARINE

404 South Riberia Street
St Augustine
FLA 32084
USA
Tel:+1 904 824 4394
Fax:+1 904 824 9755
Email: staugmar@atlantic.net

**YARD FACILITIES**

| Type | Max length | Max beam | Max weight | Max draught |
|---|---|---|---|---|
| Slipway | 38m (125ft) | | 175t | 2.7m (9ft) |
| Mobile lift | 32m (105ft) | | 110t | 3.6m (12ft) |
| Crane | | | 18t | |
| Serviced quay space | 38m (125ft) | | | 3.6m (12ft) |

**SERVICES OFFERED**

| Hull & structural work in: | Engineering | Fitting-out work | Exterior work | Exterior painting |
|---|---|---|---|---|
| Steel, aluminium, wood, composite plastics | Pipework, tanks, electrical & wiring, machinery overhaul & repair, shafts & propellers | Joinery, furnishings, interior finishing, electronics, TV, Satcom, sourcing/ supply of fittings | Bottom cleaning & painting, deck refinishing, woodwork, sanding & varnishing | In dry dock ashore under cover |

## SALTHOUSE BOATBUILDERS LTD

84 Rame Road
Greenhithe
Auckland
New Zealand
Tel:+64 9 4 139 021
Fax:+64 9 4 139 023
Email: salthouseboats@xtra.co.nz

**YARD FACILITIES**

| Type | Max length | Max beam | Max weight | Max draught |
|---|---|---|---|---|
| Slipway | 30m (98ft) | 7.9m (26ft) | 90t | 3m (10ft) |
| Serviced quay space | 43m (140ft) | | | 3m (10ft) |

**SERVICES OFFERED**

| Hull & structural work in: | Engineering | Fitting-out work | Exterior work | Exterior painting |
|---|---|---|---|---|
| Steel, aluminium, wood, composite plastics | Pipework, tanks, electrical & wiring, machinery overhaul & repair, shafts & propellers | Joinery, furnishings, interior finishing, electronics, TV, Satcom, sourcing/ supply of fittings | Bottom cleaning & painting, deck refinishing, woodwork, sanding & varnishing | Afloat ashore under cover |

## SAMOS SRL

via al Molo Vecchio
Calata Gadda
16128 Genova Porto
Italy
Tel:+39 010 254 1164
Fax:+39 010 254 1081
Email: info@samos.it

### YARD FACILITIES

| Type | Max length | Max beam | Max weight | Max draught |
|---|---|---|---|---|
| Dry dock (public) | 200m (656ft) | 15m (49ft) | | 10m (33ft) |
| Crane | | | 50t | |

### SERVICES OFFERED

| Hull & structural work in: | Engineering | Fitting-out work | Exterior work | Exterior painting |
|---|---|---|---|---|
| Steel, aluminium, wood, composite plastics | Pipework, tanks, electrical & wiring, machinery overhaul & repair, shafts & propellers | Joinery, furnishings, interior finishing, electronics, TV, Satcom, sourcing/ supply of fittings | Bottom cleaning & painting, deck refinishing | In dry dock |

## Fr SCHWEERS GMBH

Bardenfleth
27804 Berne 2
Germany
Tel:+49 421 67455
Fax:+49 421 67429

### YARD FACILITIES

| Type | Max length | Max beam | Max weight | Max draught |
|---|---|---|---|---|
| Syncrolift | 60m (197ft) | | 600t | 4m (13ft) |
| Serviced quay space | 60m (197ft) | | | |

### SERVICES OFFERED

| Hull & structural work in: | Engineering | Fitting-out work | Exterior work | Exterior painting |
|---|---|---|---|---|
| Steel, aluminium | Pipework, tanks, electrical & wiring, machinery overhaul & repair, shafts & propellers | Joinery, furnishings, interior finishing, electronics, TV, Satcom, sourcing/ supply of fittings | Bottom cleaning & painting, deck refinishing, woodwork, sanding & varnishing | Ashore under cover |

## SENSATION NEW ZEALAND LTD

11 Selwood Road
Henderson
Auckland
New Zealand
Tel:+64 9 837 2210
Fax:+64 9 836 1775
Email: refit@sensation.co.nz

### YARD FACILITIES

| Type | Max length | Max beam | Max weight | Max draught |
|---|---|---|---|---|
| Slipway | 73m (240ft) | (Unlimited) | 400t | 3m (10ft) |
| Crane | | | 250t | |

### SERVICES OFFERED

| Hull & structural work in: | Engineering | Fitting-out work | Exterior work | Exterior painting |
|---|---|---|---|---|
| Steel, aluminium, wood, composite plastics | Pipework, tanks, electrical & wiring, machinery overhaul & repair, shafts & propellers | Joinery, furnishings, interior finishing, electronics, TV, Satcom, sourcing/ supply of fittings | Bottom cleaning & painting, deck refinishing, woodwork, sanding & varnishing | Ashore under cover |

## SOUTHAMPTON YACHT SERVICES LTD

Saxon Wharf
Lower York Street
Northam
Southampton
SO14 5QF
UK
Tel:+44 (0)2380 335266
Fax:+44 (0)2380 634275
Email: sales@southamptonyachtservices.co.uk

### YARD FACILITIES

| Type | Max length | Max beam | Max weight | Max draught |
|---|---|---|---|---|
| Dry dock | 54m (177ft) | 12m (39ft) | | 3.8m (12ft) |
| Mobile lift | | 9.5m (31ft) | 200t | 4.5m (15ft) |
| Serviced quay space | 60m (197ft) | | | 4.5m (15ft) |

### SERVICES OFFERED

| Hull & structural work in: | Engineering | Fitting-out work | Exterior work | Exterior painting |
|---|---|---|---|---|
| Steel, aluminium, wood, composite plastics | Pipework, tanks, electrical & wiring, machinery overhaul & repair, shafts & propellers | Joinery, furnishings, interior finishing, electronics, TV, Satcom, sourcing/ supply of fittings | Bottom cleaning & painting, teak decking, refinishing, woodwork, sanding & varnishing | In covered dry dock ashore under cover |

## SOUTHBAY BOAT YARD

997 G Street
Chula Vista, CA 91910
USA
Tel:+1 619 427 6767
Fax:+1 619 427 0324
Email: Neil@southbayboatyard.com

### YARD FACILITIES

| Type | Max length | Max beam | Max weight | Max draught |
|---|---|---|---|---|
| Dry dock | 91m (300ft) | 23m (75ft) | | 5.5m (18ft) |
| Slipway | 91m (300ft) | | 800t | 6m (20ft) |
| Mobile lift | 21m (70ft) | | 70t | 4.3m (14ft) |
| Crane | | | 35t | |
| Serviced quay space | 55m (180ft) | | | 4.3m (14ft) |

### SERVICES OFFERED

| Hull & structural work in: | Engineering | Fitting-out work | Exterior work | Exterior painting |
|---|---|---|---|---|
| Steel, aluminium, wood, composite plastics | Pipework, tanks, electrical & wiring, machinery overhaul & repair, shafts & propellers | Joinery, furnishings, interior finishing, electronics, TV, Satcom, sourcing/ supply of fittings | Bottom cleaning & painting, deck refinishing, woodwork, sanding & varnishing | Afloat in dry dock ashore under cover |

## THEILEN NAVAL ENGINEERING SL

Furio 2
07014 Palma de Mallorca
Spain
Tel:+34 971 289070
Fax:+34 971 457592
Email: theilen@teleline.es

### YARD FACILITIES

| Type | Max Length | Max beam | Max weight | Max draught |
|---|---|---|---|---|
| Mobile lift | | | 150t | |

### SERVICES OFFERED

| Hull & structural work in: | Engineering | Fitting-out work | Exterior work | Exterior painting |
|---|---|---|---|---|
| | Pipework, tanks, electrical & wiring, machinery overhaul & repair, shafts & propellers | | | |

## TOWNSEND BAY MARINE

919 Haines Place
Port Townsend
Washington
USA
Tel:+1 360 385 6632
Fax:+1 360 385 6652
Email: jhooper@townsendbay.com

### YARD FACILITIES

| Type | Max Length | Max beam | Max weight | Max draught |
|---|---|---|---|---|
| Mobile lift | 49m (160ft) | | 300t | 4m (12ft) |
| Crane | | | 30t | |
| Serviced quay space | 50m (165ft) | 4m (12ft) | | |

### SERVICES OFFERED

| Hull & structural work in: | Engineering | Fitting-out work | Exterior work | Exterior painting |
|---|---|---|---|---|
| Wood, composite plastics | Pipework, tanks, electrical & wiring, machinery overhaul & repair, shafts & propellers | Joinery, furnishings, interior finishing, electronics, TV Satcom, sourcing/ supply of fittings | Bottom cleaning & painting, deck refinishing, woodwork sanding & varnishing | Afloat ashore under cover |

## TROPICAL REEF SHIPYARD PTY LTD

1 Fearnley Street
Portsmouth 4870
Australia
Tel:+617 4051 6877
Fax:+617 4051 0798
Email: trshipyard@iig.com.au

### YARD FACILITIES

| Type | Max Length | Max beam | Max weight | Max draught |
|---|---|---|---|---|
| Dry dock | 30m (98ft) | 9m (30ft) | | 4m (13ft) |
| Slipway | 100m (328ft) | 20m (66ft) | | 7.4m (24ft) |
| Crane | | | 90t | |
| Serviced quay space | | | | |

### SERVICES OFFERED

| Hull & structural work in: | Engineering | Fitting-out work | Exterior work | Exterior painting |
|---|---|---|---|---|
| Steel, aluminium, wood, composite plastics | Pipework, tanks, electrical & wiring, machinery overhaul & repair, shafts & propellers | Joinery, furnishings, interior finishing, electronics, TV, satcom, sourcing/supply of fittings | Bottom cleaning & painting, deck refinishing, woodwork sanding & varnishing | Afloat in dry dock |

## VITTERS SHIPYARD BV

Stouweweg 33
8064 PD Zwartsluis
The Netherlands
Tel:+31 38 3867145
Fax:+31 38 3868433
Email: info@vitters.com

### YARD FACILITIES

| Type | Max length | Max beam | Max weight | Max draught |
|---|---|---|---|---|
| Dry dock | 55m (180ft) | 12.5m (41ft) | | 3.5m (11ft) |
| Slipway | 55m (180ft) | 12.5m (41ft) | 600t | 3.5m (11ft) |
| Mobile lift | 55m (180ft) | | 600t | 6m (20ft) |
| Crane | | | 260t | |
| Serviced quay space | 55m (180ft) | | | 6m (20ft) |

### SERVICES OFFERED

| Hull & structural work in: | Engineering | Fitting-out work | Exterior work | Exterior painting |
|---|---|---|---|---|
| Aluminium, composite plastics | Pipework, tanks, electrical & wiring, machinery overhaul & repair, shafts & propellers | Joinery, furnishings, interior finishing, electronics, TV, Satcom, sourcing/ supply of fittings | Deck refinishing, woodwork, sanding & varnishing | Ashore under cover |

## VOSPER THORNYCROFT (UK) LTD

Victoria Road
Woolston
Southampton
Hants SO19 9RR, UK
Tel:+44 (0)23 80445144
Fax:+44 (0)23 80685913
Email: 106030.2263@Compuserve.com

### YARD FACILITIES

| Type | Max length | Max beam | Max weight | Max draught |
|---|---|---|---|---|
| Slipway | 120m (394ft) | | 2,000t | 4m (13ft) |
| Syncrolift | 65m (213ft) | | 1,000t | 4m (13ft) |
| Crane | | | 70t | |
| Serviced quay space | 120m (394ft) | | | 4.4m (14ft) |

### SERVICES OFFERED

| Hull & structural work in: | Engineering | Fitting-out work | Exterior work | Exterior painting |
|---|---|---|---|---|
| Steel, aluminium, wood, composite plastics | Pipework, tanks, electrical & wiring, machinery overhaul & repair, shafts & propellers | Joinery, furnishings, interior finishing, electronics, TV, Satcom, sourcing/ supply of fittings | Bottom cleaning & painting, deck refinishing, woodwork, sanding & varnishing | Afloat ashore under cover |

## W SERVICE

Testata Molo Zona 7/8
Porto Di Savona
17100 Savona
Italy
Tel:+39 019 848 5379
Fax:+39 019 848 7527
Email: info@w-service.com

### YARD FACILITIES

| Type | Max Length | Max beam | Max weight | Max draught |
|---|---|---|---|---|
| Crane | | | 280t | |
| Serviced quay space | 60m (197ft) | | | 10m (33ft) |

### SERVICES OFFERED

| Hull & structural work in: | Engineering | Fitting-out work | Exterior work | Exterior painting |
|---|---|---|---|---|
| Steel, aluminium, wood, composite plastics | Pipework, tanks, electrical & wiring, machinery overhaul & repair, shafts & propellers | Joinery, furnishings, interior finishing, electronics, TV, Satcom, sourcing/supply of fittings | Bottom cleaning & painting, deck refinishing, woodwork, sanding & varnishing | Afloat ashore under cover |

## WARREN YACHTS P/L

No 1 Kerta Road
Kincumber
NSW 2251
Australia
Tel:+61 2 436 81722
Fax:+61 2 436 81263

### YARD FACILITIES

| Type | Max length | Max beam | Max weight | Max draught |
|---|---|---|---|---|
| Slipway | 30m (98ft) | No limit | 100t | 2m (7ft) |
| Syncrolift | 60m (197ft) | 12m (40ft) | 1000t | No limit |

### SERVICES OFFERED

| Hull & structural work in: | Engineering | Fitting-out work | Exterior work | Exterior painting |
|---|---|---|---|---|
| Composite plastics | Pipework, tanks, electrical & wiring, machinery overhaul & repair, shafts & propellers | Joinery, furnishings, interior finishing, electronics, TV, Satcom, sourcing/ supply of fittings | Bottom cleaning & painting, deck refinishing, woodwork, sanding & varnishing | Ashore under cover |

## WATERSHED

c/o David Goddard
46 Quai François Mitterand
13600 La Ciotat
France
Tel:+33 4 42 08 25 76
Fax:+33 4 42 08 52 55

**YARD FACILITIES**

| Type | Max length | Max beam | Max weight | Max draught |
|---|---|---|---|---|
| Dry dock | 300m (984ft) | 30m (100ft) | | 10m (30ft) |
| Slipway | 40m (131ft) | | 150t | 3m (10ft) |
| Crane | | | 600t | |
| Serviced quay space | 1.5km (4,920ft) | | | 10m (33ft) |

**SERVICES OFFERED**

| Hull & structural work in: | Engineering | Fitting-out work | Exterior work | Exterior painting |
|---|---|---|---|---|
| Steel, aluminium, wood, composite plastics | Pipework, tanks, electrical & wiring, machinery overhaul & repair, shafts & propellers | Joinery, furnishings, interior finishing, electronics, TV, Satcom, sourcing/ supply of fittings | Bottom cleaning & painting, deck refinishing, woodwork, sanding & varnishing | Afloat in dry dock in covered dry dock |

## WAVEMASTER INTERNATIONAL PTY LTD

500, Cockburn Road
Henderson, WA 6166
Tel:+618 9 410 1422
Fax:+618 9 410 2089

**YARD FACILITIES**

| Type | Max Length | Max beam | Max weight | Max draught |
|---|---|---|---|---|
| Dry dock (under cover) | 65m (213ft) | 18m (59ft) | | |

**SERVICES OFFERED**

| Hull & structural work in: | Engineering | Fitting-out work | Exterior work | Exterior painting |
|---|---|---|---|---|
| Aluminium | Pipework, tanks, electrical & wiring, shafts & propellers | Joinery, furnishings, interior finishing | Bottom cleaning & painting, woodwork, sanding & varnishing | Afloat in dry dock ashore under cover |

## WAYFARER MARINE CORPORATION

PO Box 677
Sea Street
Camden
Maine 04843
USA
Tel:+1 207 236 4378
Fax:+1 207 236 2371
Email: wayfarer@midcoast.com

**YARD FACILITIES**

| Type | Max length | Max beam | Max weight | Max draught |
|---|---|---|---|---|
| Slipway | 38m (125ft) | | 110t | 4.3m (14ft) |
| Hydraulic trailers | | | 80t & 30t | |
| Mobile lift | 27m (90ft) | | 80t | 3.9m (13ft) |
| Crane | | | 25t | |
| Serviced quay space | 183m (600ft) | | | 5.2m (17ft) |

**SERVICES OFFERED**

| Hull & structural work in: | Engineering | Fitting-out work | Exterior work | Exterior painting |
|---|---|---|---|---|
| Steel, aluminium, wood, composite plastics | Pipework, tanks, electrical & wiring, machinery overhaul & repair, shafts & propellers | Joinery, furnishings, interior finishing, electronics, TV, Satcom, sourcing/ supply of fittings | Bottom cleaning & painting, deck refinishing, woodwork, sanding & varnishing | Afloat ashore under cover |

## NORMAN R WRIGHT & SON PTY LTD

19 Byron Street
Bulimba
Brisbane, Queensland
Australia 4171
Tel:+61 7 3399 3911
Fax:+61 7 3899 1179
Email: nrwsons@gil.com.au

**YARD FACILITIES**

| Type | Max length | Max beam | Max weight | Max draught |
|---|---|---|---|---|
| Slipway | 32m (105ft) | | 125t | 3m (10ft) |
| Serviced quay space | 32m (105ft) | | | 3m (10ft) |

**SERVICES OFFERED**

| Hull & structural work in: | Engineering | Fitting-out work | Exterior work | Exterior painting |
|---|---|---|---|---|
| Aluminium, wood, composite plastics | Pipework, tanks, electrical & wiring, machinery overhaul & repair, shafts & propellers | Joinery, furnishings, interior finishing, electronics, TV, Satcom, sourcing/ supply of fittings | Bottom cleaning & painting, deck refinishing, woodwork, sanding & varnishing | Ashore under cover |

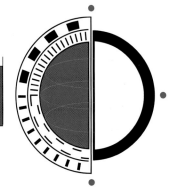

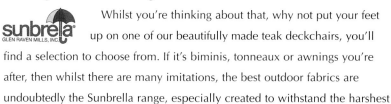

# THE SERVICES
# DIRECTORY

# A

## ABSOLUTE YACHTING
Federico Garcia Lorca 8, Son Armadams
07014 Palma de Mallorca, Spain
Tel:+34 971 738 427
Fax:+34 971 780 251
Email: info@absoluteyachting.com
• Provider of a website specifically
aimed at the yacht industry

## ACASTIMAR SL
Doctor Fleming No 3
43850 Cambrils
Tarragona, Spain
Tel:+34 977 362118
Fax:+34 977 362687
Email: acastimar@acastimar.com
• Distributor of mechanical and electrical equipment
for yachts. Agents for Cruisair air-conditioning,
Frigomatic refrigeration, Tecnicomar & Livol
watermakers, Sigmar boilers, Max Power and Super
Power thrusters, Frigonautica & Vitrofrigo fridges
and freezers, Stamegna, Paguro & Northern Lights
ac generating sets, J-prop vp propellers

## ALEXSPARES
14a High Street
Battle, East Sussex
TN33 0AE, UK
Tel:+44 (0)1424 774 888
Fax:+44 (0)1424 774 766
Email: simon@alexspares.com
• Offers a purchasing service for spare parts and
equipment for cruising yachts worldwide. All kinds
of engine parts and spares, tools, deck equipment,
fire pumps and a full range of safety equipment

## ALLAN REVIVAL SL
B-07786171, C/ Islas Baleares 41
Poligono Son Bugadellas 07180
Santa Ponsa
Mallorca, Spain
Tel:+34 971 692 919
Fax:+34 971 695 611
Email: revival@ocea.es
• Specialist in refinishing both exteriors and interiors.
Also sourcing/supply of furnishing and fittings

## ALLESTIMENTI TECNICI NAUTICI
Molo Giano – 16128 Genovo Porto
Italy
Tel:+39 010 2470941
Fax:+39 010 2470669

## ANDRAWIS YACHTS – MDI
3821 NE12 Terrace, Pompano Beach
FL 33064, USA
Tel/Fax/voice:+1 954 785 6893
Email: phil8ships@aol.com
• Specializing in total yacht refit – interior renovation
& design – yacht extensions – vessel conversions
and remodelling – project management & consulting
• Current projects include interior refit for 29m (96ft),
extending a 27m (88ft) yacht to add fishing cockpit &
swim platform

## ARDEO DESIGN
355 Ericksen Ave
Suite 421
Bainbridge Island
WA 98110
USA
Tel:+1 206 855 9027
Fax:+1 206 855 9028
Email: Scott@ardeodesign.com
• Complete yacht interior and exterior design services

## ASHBY-LIST (SPECIALIST INTERIORS) LTD
2/18 Chelsea Harbour Design Centre
Chelsea, London
SW10 0XE, UK
Tel:+44 (0)20 7352 3370
Fax:+44 (0)20 7823 3080
Email: ashby.list@telinco.co.uk
• Interior design and bespoke furniture

## ATLAS ENERGY SYSTEMS
5101 NW 21st Avenue
Suite 520
Fort Lauderdale
FL 33309, USA
Tel:+1 954 735 6767
Fax:+1 954 735 7676
• Manufactures and distributes one of the
most complete and extensive lines of energy
products worldwide. Atlas' primary products
are the unique ShorPOWER frequency and power
conversion systems and the TecPOWER marine
electrical switchboard

# B

## BACHMANN MARINE SERVICES LTD
PO Box 175, Frances House
Sir William Place
St Peter Port, Guernsey, CI
Tel:+44 (0)1481 723573
Fax:+44 (0)1481 711353
Email: james@bachmanngroup.com
• Provides services to yacht owners for registration,
radio licensing, insurance, radio traffic accounting
and VAT planning

## ARTHUR BARBEITO DESIGN
4967 SW74 CT
Miami, FL 33155, USA
Tel:+1 305 669 3211
Fax:+1 305 669 3228

## JONATHAN QUINN BARNETT
116 Vine Street
Seattle, WA 98121, USA
Tel:+1 206 322 2152
Fax:+1 206 322 2153
Email: info@jqbltd.com
• Seattle-based yacht design firm providing
interior and exterior design services. Specialist
in design solutions for custom and production
new-builds and refits over 30m (100ft). Recent
projects:30m (100ft) *Discovery*, 30m (100ft)
*Barbarina*, 36m (118ft) *Regency*

## BELINA METAL WORKS, INC
4540 South Adams Street
Tacoma
WA 98409
USA
Tel:+1 253 474 0908
Fax:+1 253 474 1560
Email: bcg@belinainteriors.com
• Belina Metal Works applies superb craftsmanship
to top designers' concepts. With master machinists,
fabricators, woodworkers, finishers and
upholsterers, the company creates unique and
exquisitely detailed custom stairways, handrail
systems, lighting fixtures and furniture, including its
electric Hi-Low table pedestals

## BENCHMARK INTERNATIONAL LTD
Quinn Close, Seven Stars Estate
Coventry CV3 4LH, UK
Tel:+44 (0)24 7630 3333
Fax:+44 (0)24 7630 3700
Email: Benchmark.Intl@cwcom.net
• Construction of interiors: joinery, furnishings,
interior finishing, sourcing/supply of fittings

## BRANDT
Anlagenbau, Teufelsmoorstr 9
D-27711 Osterholz-Scharmbeck, Germany
Tel:+49 4796 216; Fax:+49 4796 1211
Email: ulrichmoorteufel@t-online.de
• Developer and producer of cleaning machines
for applications, including cleaning of vacuum
toilet pipes

## NIGEL BURGESS LTD
16/17 Pall Mall, London SW1Y 5LU, UK
Tel:+44 (0)20 7766 4300
Fax:+44 (0)20 7766 4329
Email: london@nigelburgess.com
ALSO: Monte Carlo Sun, 74 bd d'Italie
MC 98000, Monaco
Tel:+377 9797 8121
Fax:+377 9797 8125
Email: monaco@nigelburgess.com
ALSO: 801 Seabreeze Boulevard
Bahia Mar Yachting Center
Fort Lauderdale, FL 33316, USA
Tel:+1 954 525 1090
Fax:+1 954 525 0297
Email: ftlaud@amels.nigelburgess.com
• More than 10 years' experience in providing
project management services for conversions, refits,
repairs and new building. Services include contract
negotiation, design and specification compilation,
shipyard and facility arrangements, project supervision
and management of the completed vessel

## FELIX BUYTENDIJK YACHT DESIGN
Uiterdijk 13, 4011 ET Zoelen, The Netherlands
Tel:+31 344 682596
Fax:+31 344 682595
Email: fbdesign@worldonline.nl
• Provides a worldwide design service in the field
of complete interior and exterior refits, including the
necessary adjustments to comply with the latest
rules for safety and structural fire protection. Recent
project: extension and complete refit of MY *Shark* into
44m (144ft) *No Lose* at Astilleros de Mallorca

# C

## C & C DESIGNS
George Edwards Road
Fakenham, Norfolk
NR21 8NL, UK
Tel:+44 (0)1328 855396
Fax:+44 (0)1328 855932
• Specialist in manufacturing and fitting-out marine and land-based projects

## C-TEC SA
Club de Mar s/n
E-07015 Palma de Mallorca
Spain
Tel:+34 971 405 712
Fax:+34 971 405 752
Email: c-tec_sa@2001.es
• Diesel engines, transmissions, gearboxes, electrics specialists

## CAMPER & NICHOLSONS INTERNATIONAL
12 Avenue de la Liberation
06600 Antibes, France
Tel:+33 492 912 909
Fax:+33 492 912 904
Email: info@mon.cnyachts.com
• The Yacht Management Division of CNI offers a full refit and repair service, choosing and supervising shipyards and designers, preparing specifications and overseeing implementation and cost control. MCA work is a speciality of our in-house naval architect. Recent jobs include *Mikado, Land's End, Kahlani, King, Miss Evie, Louisianna,* and *Pamina*

## CARBOSPARS LTD
Poligono Son Nougera: Solar A-9
Llucmajor, Majorca, Spain
Tel:+34 971 664 327
Email: carbospars@compuserve.com
• Supplies a comprehensive design consultancy and carries out refurbishment (or replacement with new) composite/carbon-fibre spars or other structures such as radar masts

## CARTER GREEN/SPINNEYBECK LEATHER
1 Knockhundred Row, Midhurst, West Sussex, UK
Tel:+44 (0)1730 817723
Fax:+44 (0)1730 817744
• Supplier of premium quality full grain upholstery leather in 16 finishes and a total of 600 colours from stock

## TONY CASTRO LTD
Rio House, 76 Satchell Lane
Hamble, Southampton
Hants SO31 4HL, UK
Tel:+44 (0)23 8045 4722
Fax:+44 (0)23 8045 6011
Email: tonycastro@tonycastro.co.uk
• Naval architects, yacht designers, industrial designers and engineers. Full service for sail and power including help with MCA certification, hull or superstructure changes, styling proposals with 3D renderings and computer visualizations. Twenty years' experience of innovative design and professional service

## CELI SPA
05039 Stroncone
Terni
Italy
Tel:+39 0744 607647
Fax:+39 0744 607963
Email: celispa@tin.it

## CENTOR INSURANCE & RISK MANAGEMENT LTD
9 Bonhill Street
London, EC2A 4PE, UK
Tel:+44 (0)20 7256 7300
Fax:+44 (0)20 7256 9455
Email: yacht@centor.co.uk
• Provision of complete insurance packages for yachts, their owners, guest & crew. Contacts: Mark Feltham or Simon Ballard

## CINCINNATI GEAR COMPANY
5657 Wooster Pike
Cincinnati, OH 45227
USA
Tel:+1 513 271 7700
Fax:+1 859 578 0408
Email: marinesales@cintigear.com
• In addition to manufacturing high-performance marine gearboxes and power transmission components, Cincinnati Gear provides a worldwide custom repair and rebuild service. The company's unsurpassed product quality and service expertise assures customers quick and reliable service

# D

## D&B TECHNOLOGY GROUP
1400 South Orlando Avenue, Suite 210
Winter Park 32789, USA
Tel:+1 407 647 7500
Fax:+1 407 647 7505
Email: bgravely@hoteyenow.com

## DAHLBERG SA
Nicolau de Pacs
32 Bajos, 07006 Palma de Mallorca
Spain
Tel:+34 971 774 751
Fax:+34 971 771 458
Email: dahlberg@dahlberg-sa.com
• Electronic specialist; importer of B&G, Yeoman, Tactick and Sealand (Vacuflush and sanitary systems), Dealers for Furuno in Majorca

## DAHM INTERNATIONAL
Edificio OTP, Muelle Viejo
E-07012, Palma de Mallorca, Spain
Tel:+34 971 725 246
Fax:+34 971 725 247
Email: service@dahm-international.com
And Dahm International SARL
13, Avenue du 11 November
F-06600 Antibes, France
• Offers a full range of maintenance and repair works including guarantee work for different shipyards as well as design, engineering and consulting for refits and reconstructions for sailing and motor yachts between 23 & 35 metres. Official Azimut dealer and service point for the Balearics

## DANBRIT
Ctra Andratx 26
Portals Nous
07181 Calvia, Mallorca
Spain
Tel:+34 971 677 201
Fax:+34 971 677 328
Email: danbrit@ocea.es
• Supplier and installer of electronics, TV and Satcom equipment

## GUIDO DE GROOT DESIGN
Hogewoerd 122, 2311 HT Leiden
The Netherlands
Tel:+31 (0)71 566 3040
Fax:+31 (0)71 566 3039
Email: guido@degroot-design.demon.nl
• Specialist in the design of innovative interiors and exteriors for both luxury motor yachts and sailing yachts, with experience in refits, restylings, refurbishments and conversions

## DESIGN UNLIMITED
Lakeside Studio
Carron Row Farm
Segensworth Road
Titchfield,
Fareham, Hants
PO15 5DZ, UK
Tel:+44 (0)1329 847 712
Fax:+44 (0)1329 841 068
Email: mark.tucker@designunlimited.net
• Studio specializing in interior & exterior design & styling of sailing yachts, motor yachts, refits and new builds

## DE VOOGT YACHT SERVICES BV
Vlietweg 13
2323 LA Leiden
The Netherlands
Tel:+31 (0)71 572 2230
Fax:+31 (0)71 572 1150
Email: yachtservice@fdevoogt.nl
• Offer consultancy, design and engineering services specifically for yacht conversion/refit. Can provide design calculations and steelwork, outfitting, mechanical, piping, electrical and interior drawings including technical assistance and supervision at the yard. Calculations and drawings for classification or registration with ABS, LRS, GL, BV and MCA. Technical details of all Feadships built are available. Recent refits include *Ice Bear, Mayan Queen, L'Elégance* and *Liberty GB*

## GERARD DIJKSTRA & PARTNERS
Hoogle Kadijk 147C
Amsterdam 1018BJ
The Netherlands
Tel:+31 (0)20 670 9533
Fax:+31 (0)20 675 3118
Email: info@gdnp.nl
• Naval architects specializing in large classic sailing yachts and full-rigged ships, historic, near-historic and 'spirit of tradition' refits. Major refits include *Nordwind, Endeavour, Velsheda, Shamrock V, Lulworth, Adix* and many others

## DJURGARDSVARVET

Stiebergsgatan 23
116 28 Stockholm, Sweden
Tel:+46 864 19671
Fax:+46 864 30587

## DOYLE SAILMAKERS

Marblehead, USA
Tel:+1 781 639 1490
Fax:+1 781 639 1497
Email: doyle@doylesails.com
• Premier sailmakers with representatives in over 20 countries

## DSG ASSOCIATES

4511 DuBois Drive
Vancouver
Washington 98661
USA
Tel:+1 360 735 1638
Fax:+1 360 735 1637
Email: mtm@dsgassociates.com
• Marine consultancy specializing in design and construction-related issues. These include styling, engineering and interior design matters as well as specification writing and review, contract writing and review, project scheduling and project coordination

# E

## E CUBED SYSTEMS SL

Calle Joan Miro 248
Cala Mayor
07015 Palma de Mallorca
Spain
Tel:+34 971 404 208
Fax:+34 971 404 431
Email: INFO@e3s.com
• The company has developed a unique knowledge of equipment and builds having worked on hundreds of yachts over 20m (66ft). Based on this we offer specialist design, new build consultancy, system integration, refit & repair services for all electronic aspects of your yacht

## EDMISTON & COMPANY

51 Charles Street
London W1J 5ES, UK
Tel:+44 (0)20 7495 5151
Fax:+44 (0)20 7495 5150
Email: yachts@edmistonet.com
• Whether for new construction or a major refit, Edmiston provides a complete range of services. Always in contact with the leading builders, naval architects, designers and technicians, they ensure that the right team of professionals is assembled to guarantee success of even the most complex project

# F

## FERRIOL PORTSERVICE

Plaza Barcelona 12-13
E-07011 Palma de Mallorca
Spain
Tel:+34 971 736 959
Fax:+34 971 281 715
• Cleans vacuum toilets, diesel tanks and air ducts

## ADRIAN J FISHER

8 Avenue Mirabeau
06600 Antibes
France
Tel:+33 493 34 65 47
Fax:+33 493 34 65 23
Email: adrianfisher@riviera.fr
• Specialized crew recruitment – worldwide. Acts as agent representing individual captains, project managers, mechanical/electrical engineers, chefs and senior interior staff; experienced advice on manning, salaries and contract negotiations. Careful, responsible placement from a comprehensive database. A professional and personal service for yacht owners, captains, managers, brokers and crew

## FLYING MACHINE GLASS

212 Piccadilly
London W1V 9LD, UK
Tel:+44 (0)20 7917 6257
Fax:+44 (0)20 7917 6258
• Supplier of architectural glass in a wide range of styles, textures and colours

## FRASER YACHTS

2230 SE 17th St
Ft Lauderdale
FL33316, USA
Tel:+1 954 463 0640
Fax:+1 954 463 1053

## FREDERICKS POWER & SAIL

201 Shipyard Way A/3
Newport Beach
California 92663, USA
Tel:+1 949 723 5330
Fax:+1 949 723 5332
Email: fredericks@mail.com
• Offers project coordination and management services for major refit or restoration of motor and sailing vessels of 32m (105ft) and longer

## FREEMAN MARINE EQUIPMENT INC

28336 Hunter Creek Road
Gold Beach
Oregon 97444, USA
Tel:+1 541 247 7078
Fax:+1 541 247 2114
• Provides quality doors, windows, hatches and portlights to the marine industry. Engineered elegance in watertight and weathertight closures, developed over 25 years

## KEN FREIVOKH DESIGN

Ash Studio
Crocker Hill
Fareham, Hants
PO17 5DP, UK
Tel:+44 (0)1329 832 514
Fax:+44 (0)1329 833 326
Email: all@freivokh.com
• Specialist in the restoration of classic yachts and motor vessels. Projects include the tug *St Eval*, the ice-breaker *Fredrikstad*, the steam yacht *Gonca* and the sail/motor yacht *Atlantide* and the ice-classed rescue vessel *Vega*. The work of the studio is distinguished by very careful attention to detail, resulting in truly unique projects

# G

## GLADE JOHNSON DESIGN INC

11820 Northup Way, Suite 220
Bellevue, WA 98005, USA
Tel:+1 425 827 1600
Fax:+1 425 827 2147
Email: GJDI@blarg.net
• Interior and exterior designer which has provided complete design services for a number of major refits. Team of 12 produces artistic conceptual drawings and highly detailed control drawings using the latest AutoCAD systems

## GLOBAL MARINE ENGINEERING LTD

Cobra House, Pindar Road
Hoddesdon, Herts EN11 0DE, UK
Tel:+44 (0)1992 300000
Fax:+44 (0)1992 462305
• Specializing in classic motor yachts from purchase to major rebuild. Providing a full service supervising shipyards and designers to MCA standards. Contract negotiation and cost control. Current project 45m (147ft) *Princess Oceana* (ex-*Khalidia*)

## GLOBAL POWER SYSTEMS

1500 Westlake Avenue North, Suite 4
Seattle, Washington, USA
Tel:+1 206 301 0515
Fax:+1 206 301 0660
• Suppliers of shore power frequency and phase converters

## GMT

Hagenbroeksesteenweg 94
2500 Lier (Antwerp), Belgium
Tel:+32 3 480 4845; Fax:+32 3 480 0801
Email: peter.tsounis@skynet.be
• Over the past 35 years, GMT has established a reputation for its superbly crafted teak decks and smoothly finished paint works. Its pre-manufactured method of laying teak decks takes nearly half the time of conventional teak-decking procedures, while its paint application methods result in the build-up of an infinitely smooth surface and a superior top-coat finish

# H

## H & M ELECTRONIC SYSTEMS GmbH

Schützenplatz 9
28790 Schwanewede-Beckedorf, Germany
Tel:+49 421 661546; Fax:+49 421 6530 543
Email: Trempnau@t-online.de
• Design and installation of systems for security, communications and entertainment

## HALYARD (M&I) LTD

Whaddon Business Park, Whaddon
Salisbury SP5 3HF, UK
Tel:+44 (0)1722 710 922
Fax:+44 (0)1722 710 975
Email: techhelp@halyard.co.uk
• Specialist in the design and manufacture of water-injected exhaust systems with production facilities to manufacture the entire system in-house to achieve the perfect, quiet, exhaust system

## HEINEN & HOPMAN ENGINEERING BV
Zuidwenk 45, 3751 CB Spakenburg
The Netherlands
Tel:+31 33 299 2500
Fax:+31 33 299 2599
Email: info@heinenhopman.com
• A leading company in the field of HVAC (heating, ventilating, air-conditioning) systems for marine application. Complete package from design, delivery, installation and commissioning plus servicing worldwide. All systems made to ISO-9000 codes. Recent jobs: 50m (164ft) *Golden Bay;* 52m (173ft) *Renalo*, 58m (190ft) *Sea Wolf;* 72m (236ft) *Montkaj*

## TIM HEYWOOD DESIGNS LTD
1E Olivers Wharf, 64 Wapping High Street
London E1 W2 PJ, UK
Tel:+44 (0)20 7481 8958
Fax:+44 (0)20 7481 4133
• Currently modifying/upgrading the interiors and exteriors of several large yachts with either completely new features or areas carefully matched to the existing ones. Projects include 73m (240ft) *Eco,* 74m (243ft) schooner *Phocea,* 50m (164ft) *Tugatsu*

## RON HOLLAND DESIGN
PO Box 23, Kinsale, County Cork, Ireland
Tel:+353 21 774 866; Fax:+353 21 774 808
Email: info@ronhollanddesign.com
• Design and supervision of conversion, refit or repair of yachts. Recent job: 33m (109ft) *Avalon* (ex-*Gleam*) at McMullen & Wing (NZ)

## HOWARD & HORSFIELD H2 DESIGN
9 Princeton Court, 53-55 Felsham Road
Putney, London SW15 1AZ, UK
Tel:+44 (0)20 8788 5008; Fax:+44 (0)20 8788 8043
Email: info@h2yachtdesign.com
• H2 offers a full interior and exterior design service and over the past six years has been involved in more than 18 refits of sailing and motor yachts. Largest to date was the 63m (207ft) *Sokar* (ex-*Jonikal*) totally refitted and extended by 5m (16ft)

## JOHN HUGHES & ASSOCIATES
Shieling, Church Hill, Redhill, Surrey RH1 3BL, UK
Tel:+44 (0)1737 644 885
Fax:+44 (0)1737 645 484
Email: hugheship@compuserve.com
• Brokers for the sale and purchase of vessels in the commercial sector specializing in vessels suitable for conversion to private yachts and mini cruise ships. Charter agents for cruise ships aimed at the corporate/incentive market

## HYAB OSMOCURE (& HYAB DRYTECH)
Huizerstraatweg 111, 1411 GM Naarden
The Netherlands
Tel:+31 (0)35 678 2489
Fax:+31 (0)35 678 2772
Email: info@hyab.com
• Osmosis treatment, especially suitable for large vessels with thick or cored GRP hulls

# I

## INTERNATIONAL COATINGS LTD
24-30 Canute Road
Southampton
Hants SO14 3PB, UK
Tel:+44 (0)23 8022 6722
Fax:+44 (0)23 8022 2090
• The largest paint manufacturer in the world. The International Superyacht System provides a complete paint range for new and refitting yachts. Worldwide availability and class-leading support service assures complete confidence in the product

# J

## J-CLASS MANAGEMENT
28 Church St
Newport, RI 02840, USA
Tel:+1 401 849 3060
Fax:+1 401 849 1642
Email: info@jclass.com

# K

## MICHAEL KIRSCHSTEIN DESIGNS
Lynton, Church Lane
Peppard
Henley on Thames, Oxon
RG9 5JN, UK
Tel:+44 (0)20 8758 1703
Fax:+44 (0)20 8232 8403
Email: mikekirschstein@cs.com
• Complete design service specializing in refit and new-build projects, working in the field of interior design and exterior styling, combining high-tech CAD design with conventional methods. Recent projects: 38.5m (126ft) *Santa Cruz Tres* and 64m (209ft) *Shahnaz*

## KOCH NEWTON & PARTNERS
Calle Porto Pi 4
E-07015 Palma de Mallorca
Spain
Tel:+34 971 700 445
Fax:+34 971 700 551
Email: info@kochnewtonandpartners.com
Tel:(USA) +1 954 525 7080
Fax:(USA) +1 954 525 7095
• Brokers and project managers

# L

## LINN PRODUCTS LTD
Floors Road
Waterfoot
Eaglesham
Glasgow G76 0EP, UK
Tel:+44 (0)141 307 7777
Fax:+44 (0)141 303 5106
Email: info@linnmarine.com
• Manufacturer of integrated total entertainment systems for multi-channel sound and cinema which are proven at sea to deliver uncompromised sound and picture quality, and are supported by expert worldwide service network

## LLOYD'S REGISTER OF SHIPPING
Passenger Ship & Special Service Craft Group
71 Fenchurch Street
London E3M 4BS, UK
Tel:+44 (0)20 7423 2950
Fax:+44 (0)20 7423 2016
Email: psg-general@lr.org
• The world's premier ship classification society and leading inspection and certification body. Provides classification and technical advisory services for Special Service Craft which includes yachts over 24m (79ft) and all types of International Rating Class Yachts

## LOHER RAUMEXCLUSIV GMBH
Wallersdorfer Strasse 17
D-94522 Wallersdorf-Haidlfing
Germany
Tel:+49 99 33 910 0
Fax:+49 99 33 910 280
Email: lohergmbh@t-online.de
• Interior refitters offering a complete service from draft sketch to finished interior ready for occupation

## J LUISE & SONS
Via Colombo 45, Naples 90133, Italy
Tel:+39 081 552 1237
Fax:+39 081 552 3450
Email: Luise@Luise.it
• Registered yacht and ship agency. Member of Federagenti-Assoagenti, PYA, ECPY, AYSS, AYP Marina Management Division
Tel:+39 081 761 1633
Fax:+39 081 247 9140

# M

## MARINE FAIRING & PAINTING LTD
11 Kendal Close, Waterlooville
Hants PO8 8ET, UK
Tel:+44 (0)23 9259 6667
Fax:+44 (0)23 9259 6667
• Fairing and painting contractors for both new and refitted vessels

## MARIOFF CORPORATION OY
PO Box 25, FIN 01511 Vantaa, Finland
Tel:+358 9 8708 5352
Fax:+358 9 8708 5399
Email: unto.vahasalo@marioff.fi
• Designs and manufactures water mist fire protection systems under the product name HI-Fog

## MARS METAL COMPANY
4130 Morris Drive, Burlington
Ontario L7L 5L6
Canada
Tel:+1 905 637 3862
Fax:+1 905 637 8841
Email: mars@bserv.com
• Manufacturers of keels for sailing yachts. Supplies over 1.7 million kg (4 million lb) of lead keels annually to sailboat manufacturers and individual owners. Custom bulb additions for draught reduction and added stability

## MELITA POWER DIESEL LTD

19 Garden Street, Gzira GZR 03, Malta
Tel:+356 330 964/982
Fax:+356 314 093
Email: Melita@maltanet.net
• Machinery overhaul and repair specialist and
MTU/DDC, ZF Marine and Allison Transmission
distributors. Other engineering work is undertaken
with good facilities: max length 155m (509ft), max
lift 8,500 tons
ALSO:

## MELITA YACHT PAINTERS LTD

• AwlGrip approved yacht painting specialist,
dealing with new construction and refit of any size.
Under-cover facilities in Malta

## MERIDIAN CHARTWARE LTD

50 Unthank Road, Norwich NR2 2RF, UK
Tel:+44 (0)1603 441 026
Fax:+44 (0)1603 765 253
E mail: enquiries@rcds.co.uk
• Provider of both software and hardware to the
marine market and primarily a developer of electronic
navigation systems. Leading product is SEAtrak which
uses ARCS (Admiralty Raster Chart Service)

## MERRITT KNOWLES DESIGN GROUP

1650 SE 17th St Causeway
Suite 210, Ft Lauderdale
FL 33316-1735, USA
Tel:+1 305 832 0108
Fax:+1 305 832 9951

## METALNOX BALEAR SL
## C/ISLAS CANARIAS

30-31, Poligono Son Bugadelles
07.1180 Santa Ponsa
Mallorca, Spain
Tel:+34 971 694 011
Fax:+34 971 695 691
Email: metalnox@metalnox.com
• Specialist in all areas of marine metalwork.
Teams travel all over Europe with compact welding
equipment to undertake work on superyachts

## METRICA INTERIOR

Bahnhofstrasse 73, D-48308 Senden
Germany
Tel:+49 2536 330900
Fax:+49 2536 330919
Email: info@metrica.de
• Specialist team ready to carry out refit and repair
work anywhere in the world. Operating in a flexible
and uncomplicated way to carry out repair, rebuild
and service requirements at a fair price. Recent jobs
include 48.7m (160ft) *Renalo,* 46m (151ft) *Ontario,*
80m (262ft) *Constellation,* 73m (240ft) *Boadicea*

## MO-TECH MOTOR BOOT TECHNIK SL

C/ Alexandre de Laborde 1
07011 Palma de Mallorca, Spain
Tel:+34 971 753 411
Fax:+34 971 297 219
• Mechanical and electrical engineers.
Distributors for Deutz and Deutz-MWM marine
engines, Fischer-Panda generators, Steyr
marine engines

## JOHN MUNFORD DESIGN

Building 2, Shamrock Quay
Northam, Southampton
Hants SO14 5QL, UK
Tel:+44 (0)23 8063 0880
Fax:+44 (0)23 8033 2117
Email: design@j-m-d.co.uk
• Internationally-known interior design
specialist involved with the largest projects.
Particularly known for classical design

# N

## NAIAD MARINE

50 Parrot Drive, Shelton
CT 06484, USA
Tel:+1 203 929 6355
Fax:+1 203 929 3594
Email: sales@naiad.com
• The leading manufacturer or roll stabilization
systems for yachts. Comprehensive hydraulic
thruster and integrated hydraulic system design and
manufacturing and custom engineered motion
control and hydraulic system solutions
ALSO

## NAIAD MARINE FLORIDA

3700 Hacienda Blvd, Suite 1
Fort Lauderdale
FL 33314, USA
Tel:+1 954 797 7566
Fax:+1 954 791 0827
Email: nmfl@nmfl.com
• High-quality on-site installation and service of roll
stabilization systems, stabilizer control upgrades,
hydraulic thrusters and integrated hydraulic systems
for all types of yacht

## NAUTI CHANDLER SL

Contramuelle Mollet 9
07012 – Palma de Mallorca, Baleares, Spain
Tel:+34 971 723 977/727 965
Fax:+34 971 723 977
• Marine paints and chandlery

## NAUTICA INTERNATIONAL INC

6135 NW 167th St E-17
Miami, FL 33015, USA
Tel:+1 305 556 5554
Fax:+1 305 557 0268
• Nautica RIBs (Rigid Inflatable Boats) are available
in 2.5m (9ft) to 10.8m (36ft) sizes with outboard,
inboard or diesel inboard with prop or jet drives.
Top quality, hand-laminated GRP, beautifully finished
and well-equipped yacht tenders, including
customized models

## NICHOLSON INTERIORS LTD

Unit 4 Imperial Park
Empress Road
St Denys, Southampton
Hants SO14 0JW, UK
Tel:+44 (0)23 8023 3722
Fax:+44 (0)23 8023 3994
Email: mail@nicholsoninteriors.com
• Specialist in joinery, furnishing and interior
finishing. A complete interior construction service

## NIRVANA SPARS BV

Kanaalweg 4, 8356 VS Blokzijl, The Netherlands
Tel:+31 527 291 555
Fax:+31 527 291 777
• Total mast equipment, spars & booms. Flush deck
hatches, furling booms, standing rigging, running
rigging, stainless steel ball-bearing sheet car
systems, stainless steel hydraulic cylinders,
stainless steel bollards, fairleads etc

## NORTH SAILS UK

9 Fielder Drive, Fareham, Hants PO14 1JE, UK
Tel:+44 (0)1329 508050
Fax:+44 (0)1329 220442
Email: dave@gb.northsails.com
• Manufacturing and service facility playing a
major role within the North SuperYacht Group.
The loft has a worldwide reputation for building
some of the best superyacht sails for some of the
most high profile and award-winning superyachts
including *Yanneke Too, Mamamouchi, Adela* and
the Aero-rigged *Jacquelina*

# O

## ØDEGAARD & DANNESKIOLD-SAMSØE A/S

Titangade 15, 2200 Copenhagen N, Denmark
Tel:+45 3531 1000
Fax:+45 3531 1001
Email: ods@oedan.dk
• Consulting engineers specializing in noise
and vibration

## OFFER & ASSOCIATES INTERNATIONAL

2945 State Road 84, Suite A1
Fort Lauderdale
FL 33312, USA
Tel:+1 954 587 0935
Fax:+1 954 587 8272
• Involved in the sale and refit and usually
extensions of large yachts. Offers a consultation
service assisting the customer with design
possibilities and yard selection. Recent projects
include lengthening of *Francine* (ex-*Sahab*) from
40m (131ft) to 44m (145ft), lengthening of *Monitor*
(ex-*Legend of Tintagel)* from 42m (139ft) to 46m
(152ft) and sale of 49m (163ft) *Braveheart*

## OLDENBURGER
## MOBELWERKSTATTEN GmbH

Sanderstrasse 21, D-49413 Dinklage
Germany
Tel:+49 4443 9720
Fax:+49 4443 972 275
Email: info@oldenburger.com
• Supplier of joinery and furnishing. Interior
finishing specialist

## OTTO PIENING GMBH

Am Altendiech 83
D-25348, Gluckstadt
Germany
Tel:+49 4124 916812
Fax:+49 4124 3716
Email: info@piening-propeller.de

# P

## PACIFIC CUSTOM INTERIORS INC
2601 W Marina Place Suite P
Seattle, WA 98199, USA
Tel:+1 206 282 5540
Fax:+1 206 282 2803
Email: paccustom@aol.com
• Interior design and upholstery

## PANTAENIUS GmbH & CO
Cremon 32, 20457 Hamburg, Germany
Tel:+49 40 370910
Fax:+49 40 37091109
ALSO
34 Quai Jean-Charles Rey
MC-98000 Monaco
Tel:+377 9798 4343
Fax:+377 9798 4340
Email: info@pantaenius.com
• Specialist in insurance of large yachts

## PATTON MARINE INC
## SURVEYORS & CONSULTANTS
PO Box 451135
Miami, FL 33245, USA
Tel:+1 305 854 3821
Fax:+1 305 854 3855
• Specialist in pre-purchase surveys, insurance claims, new construction, repairs and refits. Has performed more than 6,000 surveys, of which 500+ have been yachts over 30m (100ft)

## PESTO YACHT & SHIP AGENTS
Calata Molo Vecchio Modulo 3
16128 Genova, Italy
Tel:+39 0102 701305
Fax:+39 0102 701200
Email: pesto@pesto.it
• Yacht and ship agents with representatives throughout the Mediterranean; specialist in dockage reservations

## PINMAR SA
Contramuelle Mollet 6
07012 Palma de Mallorca
Spain
Tel:+34 971 713 744
Fax:+34 971 718 143
• Painting and paint supply service to large yacht industry with three divisions: Palma – headquarters, workshops, warehouses and marine supply shops; Barcelona – painting shed for large yachts, marine supply shops, warehouse and workshops; mobile service teams that travel the world supporting building and refit yards

## POKELA DESIGN
2907 Harborview Drive, Suite C
Gig Harbor, Washington 98335, USA
Tel:+1 253 853 4240
Fax:+1 253 853 4230

## PREMIER YACHT COATINGS
30 St James Street
London, SW1A 1HB, UK
Tel:+33 612 521 005
Fax:+33 493 188 192

## PRESTIGE INTERIORS
1951 Whitfield Park Drive
Sarasota, FL 34243, USA
Tel:+1 954 751 6232
Fax:+1 954 755 2141
• Yacht furniture

# Q

## QUANTUM MARINE ENGINEERING
4350 W Sunrise Bvd
Suite 116, Plantation
FL 33313, USA
Tel:+1 954 587 4205
Fax:+1 954 587 4259
Email: mperkins@quantumhydraulic.com
• Design/manufacture of hydraulic power units for stabilizers, thrusters, cranes, etc. Recent jobs include 52m (170ft) *Mayan Queen,* 48m (160ft) *Sea Kingdom*

# R

## RICHMAN MARINE
412 SE 17th St
Ft Lauderdale
FL 33316, USA
Tel:+1 954 462 0050
Fax:+1 954 462 0070

## ROBINSON HALLEN-BERG
2894 South Coast Highway
Laguna Beach
CA 9265, USA
Tel:+1 949 494 9951
Fax:+1 949 494 6281

## ROLLA SP PROPELLERS SA
PO Box 251
Via Silva 5
6828 Balerna
Switzerland
Tel:+41 91 695 2000
Fax:+41 91 695 2001
Email: info@rolla-propellers.ch
• The company manufactures conventional and surface-piercing propellers up to 3m (10ft) diameter in stainless steel and bronze. Services include performance and power prediction for displacement and planing craft; propeller design, estimation of complete hydrodynamic characteristics of propeller geometry and propeller cavitation characteristics through exclusive panel method programmes

# S

## SP SYSTEMS
St Cross Business Park, Newport
Isle of Wight PO30 5WV, UK
Tel:+44 (0)1983 828000
Fax:+44 (0)1983 828100
• Manufacture and supply of composite materials for construction and repair. Epoxy resins, adhesives, coatings, filling and fairing compounds, glass, carbon & aramid reinforcements, pre-pregs and application equipment. Structural engineering design in composites through sister company SP Technologies

## BIRGIT SCHNAASE INTERIOR DESIGN
Milchstrasse 21a, 20148 Hamburg
Germany
Tel:+49 40 410 7721
Fax:+49 40 410 7725
Email: info@schnaase.de
• Interior designers specializing in motor and sailing yachts of all sizes. Experienced in new building, refit, refurbishing, customizing and series projects

## SERVOWATCH SYSTEMS
Drakes Lane Industrial Estate, Boreham
Chelmsford, Essex CM3 3BE, UK
Tel:+44 (0)1245 360019
Fax:+44 (0)1245 362129
Email: sales@servowatch.com
US Office
Tel:+1 954 772 0532
Fax:+1 954 772 4817
• Supplier of computers, alarm, monitoring and control systems, security and surveillance, audio and video, fire detection, systems integration. *Georgia, Cakewalk and Timoneer* are among recent jobs

## SIKKENS YACHTPAINTS
## (AKZO NOBEL COATINGS BV)
Kleidijk 88, 3161 HJ Rhoon, Postbus 986
3160 AD Rhoon, The Netherlands
Tel:+31 10 503 3543
Fax:+31 10 503 3546

## SIMBA TECHNOLOGIES
Avenida Jaime III, 21, Edificio Nacar
Suite 205, 07012 Palma de Mallorca, Spain
Tel:+34 971 718 378
Fax:+34 971 729 083
• Design, supply and maintenance of computing and communications tools to the marine industry

## SLOANE HELICOPTERS
Aerodromo de Son Bonet
07009 Palma de Mallorca, Spain
Tel:+34 971 794 132
Fax:+34 971 608 270
Email: sloane@jet.es
• Helicopter support to the superyachts. Helicopter leasing, hire and sales. Helideck quotes and consultation. Interior refit/repair/supply

## PAOLA D SMITH & ASSOCIATES
300 Northeast 3rd Avenue
Fort Lauderdale, FL 33301, USA
Tel:+1 954 761 1997
Fax:+1 954 767 6270
Email: pds@pdsdesign.net
• Acknowledged internationally as one of the top interior design firms in the industry, Paola D Smith continues to produce award-winning designs. For over 25 years her firm has been providing complete design services including exterior styling and interior design as well as space planning for both refits and new construction of superyachts. Several new projects are under way including a 39.4m (129ft) Heesen, a 44.2m (145ft) Christensen and a new design for a 52m (170ft) motor yacht

## SOFTLINK SYSTEMS SARL

2000 rte des Lucioles
Aristote A – BP 29
06901 Sophia Antipolis, France
Tel:+33 (0) 493 204530
Fax:+33 (0) 493 200441
Email: info@softlink-systems.com
• A leading company in software development, based in Sophia Antipolis, France. V3, SoftLink Systems' Yacht Management programme, has been implemented for many years on a vast number of today's superyachts. An invaluable record, from construction onwards, V3 centralizes all the yacht's information, enabling secure and efficient access

## G SOLE & F MARQUET – YDPM

Via P Savi 371, 55049 Viareggio, Italy
Tel:+39 0584 389553
Fax:+39 0584 386358
Email: fm.marquet@tin.it
• A full package of services relating to the conversion/refit of superyachts: feasibility studies, preliminary design, shipyard qualification, support in negotiation and contracting, detailed design work including structural, naval architecture, engineering, interior decoration, lines and styling. Complete project management can be offered

## SOLENT INTERNATIONAL MARINE CONSULTANTS

10 High Street, Totton, Southampton SO40 9HN, UK
Tel:+44 (0)23 8086 6779
Fax:+44 (0)23 8087 3033
Email: solentint@aol.com
• Provides owners and captains with assistance in the preparation of professional detailed specifications and other documentation such as design calculations, drawings and contracts, supported by a full range of services from periodic surveys to full-time residential supervision and complete project management

## SOUTHERN SPARS NZ

117 Pakenham Street
Freeman's Bay
PO Box 90-238, Auckland
New Zealand
Tel:+64 9 358 3315
Fax:+64 9 358 3309
Email: info@southernspars.com
ALSO

## SOUTHERN SPARS US

2393 Heybourne Road
Minden, Nevada 89423
USA
Tel:+1 775 782 6788
Fax:+1 775 782 6799
Email: us.info@southernspars.com
• Specialist in the design and manufacture of custom and production masts, booms and rigging for racing and cruising yachts. Southern Spars Sail Management System, manual or hydraulic in-boom furling, which can be retro-fitted to existing masts. The in-boom furling system makes sail handling and reefing an easy short-handed operation on any point of sail

## SPINLOCK LTD

41 Birmingham Road
Cowes IOW, UK
Tel:+44 (0)1983 295 555
Fax:+44 (0)1983 295 542
E-mail: prosupport@spinlock.co.uk
• Experts in rope holding solutions. The special projects team provides expert deck layout proposals on request

## DONALD STARKEY DESIGNS

The Studio
2 Richmond Road
Isleworth
Middlesex TW7 7BL, UK
Tel:+44 (0)20 8569 9921
Fax:+44 (0)20 8569 9862
Email: donald_starkey_designs@compuserve.com
• Yacht desigfner; recent refits include 43m (141ft) *Honey Money* at Heesen and 44m (142ft) *Fortuna* at Vosper Thornycroft

## STERLING EUROPE NV

Hoek 76, Unit 55
2850 Boom, Belgium
Tel:+32 38 44 59 35
Fax:+32 38 44 60 36
Email: sterlac@sterlinglacquer.com
ALSO

## STERLING LACQUER MFG CO

3150 Brannon Av
St Louis, MO 63139, USA
Tel:+1 314 776 4450
Tel:+1 314 771 1858
• Paint manufacturer since 1907. Sterling linear polyurethane coatings, primers and fairing compounds form the nucleus of worldwide megayacht coating systems to cope with the many diverse construction materials being used in yacht building, including steel, aluminium, wood, composite plastics and even stainless steel and anodized aluminium

## STRUIK & HAMERSLAG BV

Industriestraat 4
3291 Strijen, The Netherlands
Tel:+31 78 674 2800
Fax:+31 78 674 1192
E-mail: info@struikandhamerslag.nl
• Market leader for refit and repair of yacht interiors. The core activities are cabinet making and joinery, but the entire interior including soft furnishing, upholstery and floor covering can be taken care of. More than 100 major projects completed.

## STUDIO SCANU

Largo Risorgimento 6
55049 Viareggio, Italy
Tel:+39 0584 943 229
Fax:+39 0584 31879
Email: studioscanu@inwind.it
• Designer for major refits, with relevant experience in MCA regulations. Recent jobs: rebuild of 38m (125ft) sloop *Shamrock V*, lengthening by 6m (20ft) of *Mystere Too* to 49m (161ft), new interior for 50m (164ft) Codecasa *Marcalan*, reconstruction and lengthening of *Taoahuya* (ex-*Defiance*)

## STUDIO VAFIADIS

8 Viale Dell'Astronomia
00144 Rome, Italy
Tel:+39 06 592 0066
Fax +39 06 592 0883
Email: vafiadis@interin.it
• A complete service of consultation, design and supervision of refits. Recently completed extensive refit of 41m (135ft) *O'rea* at Halkitis Shipyard, Perama, Greece

## SUPERYACHT TECHNOLOGIES

Suite 760
757 SE 17th St
Ft Lauderdale
Florida, USA
Tel:+1 954 581 7505
Fax:+1 954 581 7057

## SYSTEM HYGIENICS

Station Road Industrial Estate
Hailsham
East Sussex
BN27 2EY, UK
Tel:+44 (0) 1323 849988
Fax:+44 (0) 1323 849994
Email: craig.booth@systemhygienics.co.uk
• Specialist in the inspection, monitoring and cleaning of HVAC systems. Removal of grease from galley extracts and lint from laundry extracts using spark-free cleaning methods. Validation certificates issued, worldwide coverage, members of NADCA

# T

## TEAKDECKING SYSTEMS (EUROPE) LTD

Swanwick Marina
Swanwick
Southampton
Hants SO31 1ZL, UK
Tel:+44 (0)1489 571467
Fax:+44 (0)1489 885871
• Suppliers of pre-manufactured teak decks

## TECHMAN

Les Alizes, Villa D, 617 Ch des Cabots
06410 Biot, France
Tel:+33 493 655853
Fax:+33 493 655853
• Techman software for the organization and cross-reference of all elements of construction and refit management, and day-to-day running of yachts

## THEILEN NAVAL ENGINEERING SL

G/Furió, 2-07014 Palma de Mallorca, Spain
Tel:+34 971 289 070; Fax:+34 971 457 592
Email: theilen@teleline.es
• Engine manufacturers & suppliers. Engineers/engine room equipment. Fuel & lubricants. Propulsion systems. Refit & repair services. Masts & spars. Steering & stabilizers

## THIRTY SEVEN SOUTH LTD

PO Box 1874, Auckland, New Zealand
Tel:+64 9302 0178
Fax:+64 9307 0871
Email: service@37south.co.nz
• Yacht support services

## TILSE INDUSTRIE-UND SCHIFFSTECHNIK GMBH

Sottorfallee 12, D-22529 Hamburg, Germany
Tel:+49 40 56 1014
Fax:+49 40 56 3417
Email: tilse@t-online.de
• Manufacturer of Formglas Spezial toughened glass bent to shape in various colours and thicknesses. Also Timon tank gauging systems and Tankview software. Mavelco anti-marine growth and corrosion system for pipes and sea chests operates without chemicals, using cathodic principles

## TMS SWEDEN – TIGER MARINE SYSTEMS

PO Box 921 35
120 08 Stockholm, Sweden
Tel:+46 818 2010
Fax:+46 818 2013
Email: hq@tms.se
• Provides a multi-solution system for yachts, dealing with thermal insulation, resonance dampening, surface levelling, prevention of condensation and increased stiffness. TMS uses material from leading suppliers throughout the world

## TMT DESIGN DE PILLA SAGL

Via Bagutti 14, CH 6900
Lugano, Switzerland
Tel:+41 91972 1315
Fax:+41 91972 1317
• Services available include interior and exterior design, engineering, project development, workshop drawings, coordination and supervision, supply and installation of built-in furniture and refitting and maintenance

## TOP COAT YACHT REFINISHING TEAM

Club de Mar, PO Box 543
07080 Palma de Mallorca, Spain
Tel:+34 971 713 178
Fax:+34 971 712 178
• Specialist in painting and refinishing superyachts, among which are *New Horizon L*, *Acacia* and old classics such as *Aile Blanche*

## TRAMP OIL & MARINE LTD

Wells House, 15-17 Elmfield Road
Bromley, Kent BR1 1LT, UK
Tel:+44 (0)20 8315 7777
Fax:+44 (0)20 8315 7777
Email: bunkers@tramp-oil.com
• Worldwide supplier of fuels and lubricants

## TRIMAR SA

42 Grand Rue, L-1660 Luxembourg
Tel:+352 22 1535; Fax:+352 22 1537
ALSO: Le Panorama C/D
57 rue Grimaldi, MC-98000 Monaco
Tel:+377 93 30 62 50
Fax:+377 93 30 62 51
• Provides owners and professionals with independent advice on all yacht-related contractual matters and is the leading source of legal, fiscal and technical advice on commercial yachts and yachting in Europe. Specialist departments dealing with technical consulting (MCA, Luxembourg), administration of marine companies and registration of yachts

# U

## US PAINT

Bouwelven 1, Industrieszone – Kleingent, B-2280 Grobbendonk, Belgium
Tel:+32 14 230001; Fax:+32 14 230880
• Manufacturer of Awlgrip paint and associated products

# V

## VECO SPA

Via G Cantore 6-8
20034 Giussano, Milan
Italy
Tel:+39 0362 353321
Fax:+39 0362 852995
Email: c.formenti@veco,net
• Frigoboat marine refrigeration and Climma Marine air-conditioning

## VOSPER MOTION CONTROL

Northarbour Road, Cosham, Portsmouth
Hants PO6 3TL, UK
Tel:+44 (0)23 9238 3311
Fax:+44 (0)23 9232 5133
• Manufacturer of Vosper, Naiad and Koop Nautic stabilizers

# W

## WARDS MARINE ELECTRIC

630 SW Flagler Avenue, Fl 33301, USA
Tel:+1 954 523 2815
Fax:+1 954 523 1967
• Over 50 years of service to the yachting industry providing ABYC certified marine electricians for dockside assistance, engineering, electrical and corrosion surveys, computerized engraving and worldwide distribution of marine electrical parts

## WESTERBEKE CORPORATION

150 John Hancock Road, Taunton, MA 02780, USA
Tel:+1 508 823 7677
Fax:+1 508 884 9688
• Marine engines

## WHITING POWER SYSTEMS

152 Beaumont St, Westhaven
Auckland, New Zealand
Tel:+64 9 358 2050
Fax:+64 9 358 0285
Email: sales@whiting.co.nz

## ANDREW WINCH DESIGNS LTD

The Old Fire Station
123 Mortlake High Street
London SW14 8SN, UK
Tel:+44 (0)20 8392 8400
Fax:+44 (0)20 8392 8401
E-mail: info@andrew-winch-designs.co.uk
• Specializes in high-quality, versatile design of power and sailing yachts for both the custom and production boat markets

# Y

## YACHT FUEL SERVICES

37 St John's Hill
London SW11 1TT
UK
Tel:+44 (0)20 7738 2124
Fax:+44(0)20 7738 2127
Email: mail@yachtfuel.com
• A professional and reliable source of competitively priced, high-quality marine fuel and lubricants worldwide. A bunkering consultancy service giving a valuable second opinion on the availability of top-quality fuel, duty free prices and a port of call en route. Extensive credit facilities also available

## YACHT INTERIOR FURNISHINGS

5620 NW 12th Avenue
Fort Lauderdale
FL 33309
USA
Tel:+1 954 776-6350
Fax:+1 954 776 6358
Email: YIF@yacht-refit.com

## YACHT PAINT

Boero Colori srl, I – 16121 Genova
Via Macaggi 19, Italy
Tel:+39 010 5500 1
Fax:+39 010 5500 291
Email: boero@boero.it
• Yacht Paint is a division of Boero Colori, the ISO 9002 approved paint and coating manufacturer, offering a comprehensive range for the care and protection of luxury yachts. Used on more than 180 major new projects and countless refits over 20 years

## YACHTING PARTNERS INTERNATIONAL

28/29 Richmond Place
Brighton
BN2 2NA, UK
Tel:+44 (0)1273 571722
Tel (USA):+1 800 626 0019
Fax:+44 (0)1273 571720
Email: ypi@ypi.co.uk

# Advertisers Index

# Photographers